Culture of the Phalaenopsis Orchid

(First Revision, 1990)

Bob Gordon

Published by
Laid-Back Publications
Rialto, California USA

Typesetting by
Archetype Typesetting & Type Design
Riverside, California USA

Graphic Design by
Laura Landrum
Moreno Valley, California USA

Printed in Singapore
through Interprint
In collaboration with R.F. Marketing & Lithography

Library of Congress Catalogue Card Number: 85-81011

Cover: Phalaenopsis Nancy Gordon
"Shamrock"

TABLE OF CONTENTS

PHOTOS

FIGURES

To Nancy, because...

BEFORE WE GET STARTED...(Don't skip this part; it's important!)

This is the first revision of the basic book and it has been up-dated, revised and expanded and some of the dumb mistakes I made in the first edition have been corrected.

If you are now growing Phalaenopsis or are thinking about growing them, this book is for you. It's intended as sort of a volksbüch for the non-scientist grower and, to that end, is expressed in everyday, non-threatening, user-friendly language. The objective is to take some of the mystery out of growing phals and allow the grower to enjoy the flowers without having to make them a career.

It is not a scientific treatise, but on these pages the reader will find some practical guidance in Phalaenopsis culture directed toward getting him or her through the three stages of orchid learning. These are: first, keeping the plants alive; second, getting them to bloom and; third, getting them to bloom well; (there is another one...where you know 'everything there is to know' and refuse to learn anymore, but that really is a return to the first stage).

Herein, you'll find ideas for Phalaenopsis, or phal, growers at all three levels of competence. There is instruction in good culture for those who are merely interested in phals; better culture for those who are deeply involved with phals; and best culture for those who are bonkers over them.

THE IMPORTANT STUFF IS CALLED OUT IN CAPITAL LETTERS.

There is a common misconception that hobbyists cannot grow phals as well as the professionals, the reason being that the 'commercials' jealously guard their trade secrets in order to make the heaps of money we all know they have. Right? Actually, the real situation is a lot less colorful than that.

Any time a reasonably intelligent being brings a lot of attention and energy to focus on a narrow subject such as Phalaenopsis culture, he or she is going to learn a great deal about it. After grasping the basics of Phalaenopsis culture, any serious amateur should be able to do a far better job of growing them than the commercial growers.

That is so, not because the commercial growers can't, but simply because they cannot afford to commit a lot of time and expense just to get a little more quality out of a stock plant. They are more concerned with cash flow, return on investment, stock turnover, advertising, and utilities costs than they are with much beyond keeping the plants in good condition until they are sold.

IF YOU REALLY DON'T WORRY TOO MUCH OVER HOW MUCH EFFORT IT TAKES TO GET THESE LITTLE SUCKERS TO BLOOM WELL, I HAVE SOMETHING FOR YOU. READ ON.

WHY SHOULD I GROW PHALAENOPSIS? Frequently, when I talk to people about growing phals, they volunteer some negative answers to this question and the reasons for them. Most of the answers fall into one of five categories. Let's look at some of the common reasons for not growing Phalaenopsis orchids and I'll tell you why I don't think they are valid.

1.   They are finicky and difficult to grow.
2.   They are subject to diseases that don't affect other orchids.
3.   They require more heat and cost more to grow.
4.   They bloom all at once and are bare the rest of the year.
5.   They take up more bench space than other orchids.

ON NUMBER 1: Phals are no more difficult to grow than any other orchid. They simply require that you understand their needs...which are relatively simple and which are outlined in Chapter Two of this book.

ON NUMBER 2: That's partly true, but the diseases are not hard to control and all you need to know on the subject is outlined in Chapters One and Two of this book.

ON NUMBER 3: True; about 5° F. higher than cattleyas, but they also will tolerate higher temperatures in the summer, so the extra cost of heat in the winter is partially offset by the savings in cooling costs in the summer.

ON NUMBER 4: For the most part, true, spring-bloomers flower sometime between February and June, at least they do in the northern hemisphere. But, on the other hand, many mature Phalaenopsis plants will bloom for 2 to 3 months on the first blooming cycle of the growing season and another month or two after a short rest...on the so-called 'summer spikes'. How many other orchids will be in bloom for 3 or 4 months out of a year? Precious few, I think. Talk about getting your money's worth! On top of that, many of the species normally bloom in the summer and autumn. Result? Flowers year round.

Phalaenopsis flowers stay in bloom a long time. Individual flowers are in bloom on a healthy plant for an average of 35 days, but amabilis flowers last up to four months. This long-flowering habit is a feature that make the Phalaenopsis a particularly good choice for beginners with only a few plants. It also is an endearing quality to cut-flower growers. The fact that phals grow and bloom well in the home is frosting on the cake for beginners.

ON NUMBER 5: Again, partly true, but the use of step benches, as outlined in Chapter Four, more than offsets this minor disadvantage.

With regard to the general charge that phals require more care than other orchids, I direct your attention to the hoary Principle of Benign Neglect which has enjoyed so much success since man began to take charge of his environment: IF IT AIN'T BROKE, DON'T FIX IT.

Our intervention into natural processes are usually in the form of excesses. This, probably because of an innate belief that if a little is good, a lot is better. Don't you believe it. Try living by "Paucity is Perfect" and your phals (and maybe your waistline) will improve.

OK, that's all the evangelizing I'm going to do, at least for now, on behalf of "the serene beauty of the...Phalaenopsis", as Rebecca Tyson Northen so poetically puts it.

A comment on advice: If a technique that you are using now to grow your phals is working, for heaven's sake, stay with it. *Don't change,* at least not until you feel in full command of what's going on. Too many growers go willy-nilly from one potting medium to another, from one fertilizer to another, and from one pot style to another, ad nauseum. If you are hung up on trying new things, fine. Otherwise, just give it a rest and spend the time enjoying your flowers. I think it was Supreme Court Justice Learned Hand who commented "No advice is worth a damn...including this." Enough on advice.

Concerning the pesticides mentioned in this text, I have had my greatest success with the materials and methods described. However, none of this can constitute a legal recommendation. No claims are made that this is the only successful program, or that the materials are legally available for these uses. As new materials come onto the market, better alternatives may become open to the grower; however, this program has been successful for me, and can be used as a guideline for preventive maintenance with the reader's Phalaenopsis plants.

While I learned most of the lessons herein the expensive way, I do want to thank publicly all of those whose paths I've crossed in Phalaenopsis matters in recent years...for the help, the ideas, and the inspiration you've given me. You may see your ideas in print here. If you do, take a bow.

Let's get on with growing the Phalaenopsis orchid.

CHAPTER ONE

THE BASICS

Section   1. The short course. (Phal. 101)

              2. How Nature grows them.

              3. How to grow them better.

Section 1. THE SHORT COURSE

The Phalaenopsis is an ideal orchid for beginners. Most bloom in the spring and a mature plant will often stay in bloom for *3 months*! They are easy to grow in the home because if you're comfortable, so will they be. (Forgive me if I think of phals as people.) Here's how it's done:

LIGHT. They like direct, but filtered, sunlight. Ten to fifteen percent of full sunlight is what they like best. This is easy to obtain in a south or east window that has a lace curtain or a tree outside to reduce the light to the 'dappled' or 'bright shade' level. Too much light bleaches the leaves to a light green or even sunburns them. A medium green means the light level is about right. Grow them in the same location you'd grow an African violet, but do not put them in a north window. They probably will not bloom there.

HUMIDITY. High humidity is a must and something that is not common in many parts of the world or in heated/air-conditioned homes anywhere. It's easy to get, though, merely by putting the plant on a tray of wet gravel, an inch or two deep. Add water daily to keep up with evaporation losses, but don't let the pot sit in the water. Soaking-wet roots can cause rot problems.

TEMPERATURE. This one's easy. Phalaenopsis orchids like about the same temperatures that you do. Minimum temperature is 60° F. and maximum is about 85.

WATERING/FEEDING. Phals like to have their roots damp, but not wet. Does that make sense? In the summer that means watering about twice a week. Feed with quarter-strength fertilizer with every watering. For starters, almost any houseplant food will do for the phals.

AIR MOVEMENT. Gentle air movement makes the plant feel good and helps prevent disease. It also holds down leaf surface temperatures if the light gets too bright and this can prevent sunburn.

That's basically all that is involved. That's it. And you, too, can grow the serenely beautiful 'moth orchid'. It's worth knowing that most adolescent phals will have half again as many flowers which are a third larger in the second and subsequent years. You probably bought one that is blooming for the first time, so rest easy; the best is yet to come.

Section 2. HOW NATURE GROWS THEM

Most Phalaenopsis orchid species (the natural forms opposed to the man-made ones) come from the southwest Pacific area, notably Indonesia and the Republic of the Philippines. That's nice to know, but it's important, too, because the basic aim of Phalaenopsis culture is to re-create the environmental conditions, minus the harmful ones, that the original species enjoyed and which were responsible for their survival and proliferation over the thousands of years they've been around.

As soon as you can, read the literature and talk to people who grow them or have seen them in the wild. The idea is to learn their idiosyncrasies and special cultural needs. If you understand how they grow in nature, you can better meet their needs in culture. For example, Malayan violaceas tend to prosper in the wild on trees hanging over river banks.(Dourado,1978) Read: they like the extra humidity. Those found in the wild usually are tilted enough to allow rainwater to run out of their crowns, too. Keep that one in mind; the idea is to avoid water stagnation in the crown that could cause crown rot, a serious disease to the plant.

POINT: IT'S UP TO *YOU* TO ADJUST THE ENVIRONMENT TO THE PLANT'S NEEDS. DON'T EXPECT THE PLANT TO DO THE ADJUSTING. It's in charge of growing; you are in charge of letting it.

I know a local grower who had half a dozen miltonia orchids that grew and flowered well under warm, relatively dry conditions...an unusual circumstance to say the least. I asked him how he'd managed to do that and he replied that he'd had some problems and had lost some plants in trying to grow them in such dry conditions. When I asked how many he'd lost, he said "A hundred and thirty-seven; these are the survivors". The moral: Some plants probably will survive adverse growing conditions, but it's a lot more rewarding if you make a conscious effort to (1) find what they need and, (2) give it to them. Dale Carnegie advises the same principle in winning friends and influencing people, by the way. Carnegie should have grown phals.

PHALS LIKE RELATIVELY CONSTANT, WARM TEMPERATURES; MEDIUM TO HIGH HUMIDITY; MOVING AIR; RELATIVELY LOW LIGHT; FREQUENT WATERING; AND GOOD DRAINAGE. THEY ARE EPIPHYTIC, THAT IS, THEY GROW ON TREES RATHER THAN IN THE GROUND.

Providing those growing conditions doesn't sound too difficult, does it? It should be easy to re-create these conditions in the home or in a greenhouse, and it is. Let's move on to see how these needs match up with what we can provide.

Section 3. HOW TO GROW THEM BETTER

If you have progressed past the first level of skill in phal culture and feel comfortable in your ability to keep your plants alive, it's time to move up to the second level.

This time we'll use the same five basic controls we used at the first level, but we'll look at them in more detail.

Section 3.1 LIGHT CONTROL

Phals need 1,000 to 1,500 footcandles of light for good growth, depending on the season of the year. That's about 10-15% of direct sunlight in most areas where phals are grown. Getting an accurate reading of your lighting condition can be something of a problem, but there is more than one way to measure. If you have access to a direct-reading light meter that is graduated in footcandles, super. If not, perhaps you are camera-competent or know someone who is.

To read approximate light level values, set the film speed indicator on your light meter, or on the camera if it's built-in, to ASA or ISO 100. Take a *maximum* reading of the light in your growing area as it is reflected off a Kodak Neutral Test Card, the gray side. (These card sets are available, inexpensively, at almost any complete camera store or counter.)   Set the meter, if it is not automatic, and read the aperture called for opposite 1/100th of a second. Then compute:

$$\frac{1.15 \times (aperture)^2}{.1}$$

For example, if 1/100th of a second falls on an aperture of $f8$, compute $1.15 \times (8)^2$, 1.15×64 divided by $.1$ = about 736 footcandles, a tad low for most Phalaenopsis light requirements. Move to a brighter spot.

THE OLD HOME REMEDY OF HOLDING ONE HAND 12 INCHES ABOVE THE OTHER AND WATCHING FOR A HAZY SHADOW INDICATING 1,000 FOOTCANDLES IS NOT A USEFUL MEANS OF MEASURING LIGHT.

It's only accurate plus or minus 50%. When I first tried this old saw, I got what I thought was 1,000 footcandles when the light was actually anywhere from 500 to 1,500fc.

Light levels are important for growing any kind of orchid, but, if it makes you feel any better, the light meter business is alive and well and a meter made for plant culture is available. Read on.

Be aware, before you settle on how much you have in any particular spot, that sunlight reaching the earth's surface varies not only seasonally, but also with variations in air pollutants, humidity, cloud coverage, time of day, and overhead vegetation...among other things.

Take readings on several consecutive days, several months apart, to see what is happening to light levels over a whole season. It will astound you how great the difference is...and go a long way toward explaining why shading must be adjusted to get optimum growth from your phals. See Section 13 for the needed light levels and the rationale for them. (if that interests you; if not, to hell with it; they probably will do OK anyway.)

16

A passive way to gauge the light level in your growing area is to watch for long-term indications of too much light that include a yellow-green leaf color, and smaller than normal flowers on shorter than normal spikes which are short-lived.

In particular, watch a plant very closely when it is put into a questionably high light location. If the leaves get even a little bit warmer than the surrounding air temperature, the location is probably too bright. Move it right now.

Long-term indications of not enough light are easy to detect: No flowers...usually. There are exceptions, but that is usually the reason why mature, healthy phals don't bloom. Move the plant to a higher or brighter location, but do so in small steps so the plant may adjust easily to the new growing condition. Move it too quickly into a bright spot and it could get sunburned...not a serious condition, usually, but it is unsightly.

Increase air circulation around the plant when you or nature increases the light the plant gets. The leaf surfaces should always be cool to the touch. Also, increase the amount of fertilizer given to a plant along with the increase in light. It will need it. It's like going faster in your car; you need more gas. (Conversely, reduce air movement and fertilizer in the autumn when the light level goes down.)

Serious growers laughed when they first heard of a man in Southern California trying to grow quality odontoglossum orchids, which are more at home in the cool, dim greenhouses of Central Europe. Bob Dugger solved the problem of too much light by shading and increasing air circulation in his greenhouse almost to gale levels. It worked.

AIR CIRCULATION SHOULD BE MATCHED TO LIGHT LEVELS...MORE LIGHT, MORE AIR. VICE VERSA. This is an important point that will come up again, so if you didn't catch it, back up and read it again.

In the wild, some phals do very nicely on the tops of trees, in full sunlight. How do they keep from burning up? Think about it...and think of cool breezes.

How can you tell if you have enough air circulation? If leaf surface temperatures stay cool to the touch, you probably are OK. Check the plants that are in the brightest spots. Cigarette smoke should move positively around all the plants if there is enough air movement.

Incidentally, don't make a practice of smoking around *any* orchid. Tobacco mosaic virus is bad news. I'm told it isn't carried by cigarettes, but why take the chance? **AT THIS POINT, ORCHID VIRUSES CANNOT BE CURED.**

TRY FOR AT LEAST 6 HOURS OF DIRECT SUNLIGHT EACH DAY, SPRING AND FALL. Winter and summer will take care of themselves. When I say direct light, I mean just that, BUT, filtered to the 1,000 to 1,500 fc (85% shade)level; 'dappled' light or 'bright shade', if that helps any. Southern exposures in your house or greenhouse are best. East is next best, because you get light without heat. Western exposures are the third choice (they'll need more air movement here) and northern exposures are out altogether.

While it is true that phals will prosper in most places the African violets will, it does not hold true for northern exposures, which suit the African violets just fine. A few plants may bloom in a northern exposure, but you are fighting the odds.

Put your Phalaenopsis in a northern outlook and you'll produce lovely vegetation, but few flowers. (Do you remember my comment earlier that the most common cause of a phal's failure to flower...was lack of light?)

A lace curtain, a venetian blind, a sheer backing or any other such means to break the full intensity of the sunlight is what you need. If you use a south window exposure, play it safe and place the plant well back from the glass at first. See if the leaf temperature gets up to the 'warm'. Do that gradually over a period of several days to be on the safe side.

If it doesn't heat up on the surface of the leaf, move it a bit closer to the window. If you get carried away and move too quickly, the plant may suffer...with terrible finality. A small fan blowing over the top of the plant at this stage will take away some of the risk.

Watch the light level changes that occur with seasonal changes and either move the plants or increase/ decrease the shading. Better you should have too little than too much. A plant that didn't bloom this year because it didn't get enough light may bloom next year. A dead one certainly won't.

Sunburn on the 'recurve' surface of Phalaenopsis leaves is usually not fatal to the plant. I say usually because if the burned leaf happens to be the emerging new one, kiss the plant goodbye. It is in the nature of monopodial or one-footed plants, of which Phalaenopsis is one, to have only one growing leaf point. If that one is badly sunburned, the

effect is the same as crown rot, a fairly common cause of demise in phals.

Some time back, a friend gave me a 5-year old, unbloomed Phalaenopsis gigantea seedling and I sunburned the new, 1/4 inch emerging leaf by putting it in an untested location in a new greenhouse. (Note: giganteas are the tortoises of the Phalaenopsis genus. They seldom bloom earlier than 8 years from germination; 9 to 12 years is the norm on the US mainland.)

It died.

I was sick over the tragedy and I still can't bring myself to tell the friend how dumb I'd been. (If you read this, Dick, I'm sorry.)

FOR STARTERS, IT'S BETTER YOU SHOULD GIVE A PLANT TOO LITTLE LIGHT THAN TOO MUCH IN A NEW AND UNTESTED LOCATION.

Once you've grown phals in a location for a full year without harm, it's relatively safe to assume that a new one put in that spot should be OK.

Regarding location, in the home or in a greenhouse, it's probably true that if you have the wrong one, nothing you do will make the plant flower. Conversely, if you have the right one, nothing you do will *keep* it from blooming. A realtor-friend told me once that the three most important things in determining the value of a piece of property are (1) location; (2) location; and (3) location. I know there is a connection there, somewhere.

The older heads in the orchid business are fond of saying if a plant won't bloom in one spot, move it a little. They're probably right, because your greenhouse or growing area is not blessed with uniform growing conditions over its entirety. It's probably made up of a set of micro-environments, each a little different from the others, and quite possibly just what a given plant needs to thrive. That point is worth remembering:

IF A PLANT WON'T BLOOM IN ONE LOCATION, MOVE IT A LITTLE.

I'll add one qualification to that advice: Move it to a slightly brighter spot, since the usual reason why a phal won't bloom, again, that it isn't getting enough light.

Incidentally, if it is getting too much light, it probably will bloom, but the flowers will be small and short-lived. Second point here,

IF THE FLOWERS ARE SMALL AND DON'T LAST LONG, MOVE THE PLANT TO A SPOT THAT HAS A LITTLE LESS LIGHT.

Are you getting the point that light levels are important to good Phalaenopsis culture? If so, you're getting the right message. Don't be afraid to experiment a little with location and light, but when you do,

CHANGE GROWING LOCATIONS A LITTLE AT A TIME.

Try to be logical about change and make note of why you moved something. That would be the disciplined, scientific way to approach this...and the surest way to profit from your mistakes.

A few years back, a grower in the Portland, Oregon area, was given some seedlings of an intergeneric cross of cymbidium by bifrenaria,

a cross that hadn't been grown in culture before. Of course, he had no idea of its cultural needs. He put the seedlings at different locations around the greenhouse and waited.

The only one that finally bloomed was under the bench, on top of the steam pipes. There is a lesson here: Each plant you'll own probably has a 'sweet spot', hopefully, somewhere in your growing area. The challenge is to find it. Can you see why it is important to learn a little about the place the plant species came from originally?

A point worth remembering is that

BRIGHT LIGHT AND COOL TEMPERATURES OFTEN YIELD BRIGHTER COLORS IN SOME ORCHIDS.

That phenomenon probably has to do with a surplus of food generated during daylight hours that is not consumed by the plant as a result of warm nighttime conditions. Bright, cool days with cool nights makes for strong plants with brilliant colors.(Griesbach, 1983)

When a Phalaenopsis plant blooms, move it into lower light to prevent bleaching out the color and shortening flower life. More on this later.

ARTIFICIAL LIGHT.

I have not dealt with Phalaenopsis culture under artificial lighting in this book, because (1) I am not competent to do so and (2) there are already a number of adequate instruction books available to those interested. The American Orchid Society offers several publications which cover the subject authoritatively.

These include:

Growing Orchids Indoors
American Orchid Society

Handbook On Orchids
Brooklyn Botanic Garden

Orchid Culture Under Lights
Indoor Light Gardening Soc

Learn To Grow Under Fluorescent Lights
Indoor Light Gardening Soc

Light Gardening Primer
Indoor Light Gardening Soc

Light Garden Construction
Indoor Light Gardening Soc

Home Orchid Growing
Rebecca Tyson Northen

Orchids As House Plants
Rebecca Tyson Northen

The source of probably the largest number of orchid titles anywhere in the world is:

Twin Oaks Books
P.O. Box 20940
Greenfield, WI 53220

Members of the American Orchid Society may order books/pamphlets from the:

American Orchid Society
6000 South Olive Ave.
West Palm Beach FL 33405

In Australia, an excellent source of orchid books is:

Orchidaceous
P.O. Box 378
Alstonville, NSW 2477

In the UK try:

Orchid Sundries
Scotchey Lane, Stour Provost
Nr Gillingham, Dorset SP8 5LT

That's enough on light for now. Let's talk about the second requirement for growing and flowering Phalaenopsis orchids, temperature control.

Section 3.2 TEMPERATURE CONTROL.

Phalaenopsis orchids are warm-growing plants which prefer a temperature range of 62 to 85° F. That's the way they grow in nature. There will be a time, however, when the temperature should be deliberately dropped below 60 degrees to set flower spikes. This also is the way it is in nature. For the majority of the growing season, though,

MINIMUM TEMPERATURE FOR PHALS SHOULD BE HELD TO 62° F.

At the top end, 85° is the maximum desired, but temperatures up to 95° will not permanently harm the plants. Production of food, however, falls off above 85° and there is a danger of desiccating the plants or allowing leaf surface temperatures to exceed the point where irreversible damage is done.

LEAF SURFACE TEMPERATURES CAN EASILY EXCEED AMBIENT TEMPS BY 25 DEGREES OR MORE

...and not be apparent. For that reason it's best just to hold temperatures at the plant to a max of 85° F.

AND REMEMBER TO INCREASE THE AIR MOVEMENT AROUND THE PLANTS AS THE TEMPERATURE GOES UP.

You turn the fans on in the summer when *you* get warm, don't you? Same principle. Keep your plants comfortable and they'll return the favor by being beautiful.

Many of us have learned the lesson of what can happen to a Phalaenopsis plant left in a closed car on a sunny day. With the sun beating down on a dark green leaf and no air circulation, leaf temperatures can skyrocket in just minutes and your plant is fried. I left some vandas, which are normally comfortable in full sunshine *outdoors,* in a closed automobile for an hour in mid-morning in December in Hawaii. Zapped. One survived, but it was 3 years before it flowered again.(Same reason why you should never leave your pets in a closed car in the warm weather.)

The same danger exists for phals that are hung up high in a greenhouse, next to the glass. There aren't many that need that kind of light anyway, so avoid hanging or placing a phal within 12 inches of the glass at the top of a greenhouse. Number one, there's too much light there for most phals and number two, there usually isn't much air circulation up there... unless you direct your vertical air fans to blow upward. I recommend this.

Apply the same precautions to plants on benches *next to the glass*. I put some plants on a bench next to the glass one summer and had no problems with overheating... until the sun angle lowered as autumn came on and it burned every leaf that faced it. I now have shade compound on my south-facing glass, permanently, along with the shade cloth. Don't allow leaves to touch the glass, either. Good way to burn them.

Point: WATER HIGH PLANTS AND THOSE NEXT TO THE GLASS MORE OFTEN THAN THE REST.

They'll need it with the higher light and heat levels.

Light intensity falls off rapidly as you move away from the source and, in this case, the glass or plastic in the roof of a greenhouse can be considered a light source. The closer the plant is to the glass, the more often it's going to need watering. It wouldn't hurt to put these plants in a finer bark mix than the other plants at benchlevel. The fine bark dries out slower because it holds more water.

I usually save that kind of bright bench space for species like pulchras and lueddemannianas that produce keikies instead of flowering when they don't get enough light. Sometimes they will produce keikies even when they have enough, but that is in the nature of some of the leudde/pulchra species. For some reason, they don't bloom every year.

(Keiki is the Hawaiian word for child and use of the term has been adopted by most phal growers to refer to clonal growths or little plants that sometimes grow on phal flower spikes.)

FLOWERING LUEDDEMANNIANAS

To all those of you who have been frustrated by lueddemannianas over the years:

The Phalaenopsis species lueddemanniana has a peculiar flowering habit which is reminiscent of some of the big brassocattleyas in that they appear to need to reach a fairly large physical size before they will bloom well, if at all.

Growers who divide the big brassocatts before they reach that critical size (puberty?) are usually disappointed in their flowering habits. But on the other hand, if they leave the plant alone and let it get big, it will give a grower all the blooms a body could ever ask for.

Same thing with the lueddes.

Don't cut the keikis off; leave them alone and, if you want a specimen-sized plant, don't repot it, either. The plant will throw enough external roots to provide it with all the moisture-gathering capacity it needs; the roots in the pot will rot, but who the hell cares? You won't be able to see the pots, anyway. They'll be buried.

Put it up high where it gets lots of light and warmth and give it lots of water. In 2-3 years the plant should reach the critical size and, others factors allowing, will bloom and produce loads of keikis which themselves will bloom. Then you can cut a few of them off, but don't disturb the main mass of the plant.

Back to temperature control: Contrary to popular belief, healthy, happy phals never stop growing; some slow down a lot, but they don't stop growing altogether. This is characteristic of all phals so far as I know...and may be true of all tropical orchids. Why should they? It's summer most of the time where they come from. Think about it.

IF YOU ARE GROWING YOUR PHALS

IN A HOUSE OR AN APARTMENT, TEMPERATURE SHOULD NOT BE A PROBLEM,

because if you're comfortable, so will your plants be. But, be careful not to set the thermostat below 60 degrees at night. Some thermostats will go down to a temperature setting in the mid-or low-50s...and that's too low for the phals. This is especially true of some of the thermostats made in recent years.

In the winter it's well to move your plants back away from the windows to avoid cold drafts, which can be harmful to the warm-growing Phalaenopsis. The lower sun angle in the winter will tend to compensate for the set-back anyway. Drawing curtains or drapes at night will not only keep cold drafts off the phals, but will also save on your heating bill. In colder climates, you may want to consider the use of thermal shutters, shades, or curtains.(Langdon,1980)

THE PHALAENOPSIS ORCHID IS NOT A YEAR-ROUND OUTDOOR PLANT

in any US location except parts of Hawaii and Puerto Rico...and not a very good idea there, either, unless they're under cover to keep off the rain.

If you live where daily temperature extremes do not fall outside the 62 to 85° limits, and the daytime humidity does not fall below 50%, you can "summer out" your Phalaenopsis plants, or move them outdoors to give them the benefit of the, as the Brits so aptly put it, "buoyant" summer air. This is particularly well-advised for those who grow their plants under lights or in marginal lighting conditions during the rest of the year. It's like a summer vacation then back to the old grind in the autumn.

If you're going to put them outside, though, remember to keep up with the cultural requirements and bring them back indoors when temperature or humidity get outside the limits noted above. There are many sadder-but-wiser orchid growers in south Florida who have lost their outdoor plants to one of those once-in-a-century frosts that afflict the area every few years.

I know a lady grower in Orlando who, with her husband, bought a piece of property there that had a natural limestone sinkhole on it, several hundred feet across. They bought a large number of native Florida orchids and planted them in the virgin thickets around the sinkhole. A few months later, they had one of those frosts and they lost every one. Not one survived.

REGARDING HEATING SYSTEMS, even in the coldest climates,

IT IS IMPERATIVE YOU PROVIDE A CONSTANT SOURCE OF FRESH AIR TO THE GREENHOUSE.

Air in a tightly closed greenhouse becomes unhealthy very quickly for the plants. The problem usually doesn't arise, though, because most greenhouses are only loosely sealed and fresh (cold) air easily infiltrates through cracks, gaps, and other openings.

If you have a combustion heater in your greenhouse, either gas or oil, provide a conduit to bring cool, fresh air in from the outside to the combustion chamber. There is little point in heating air, then feeding it into the fire box to go out the chimney. The practice will cut down on some of the cold drafts, too.

In most combustion heaters, however, an air supply to the stack must be provided, but few, if any, heaters are made such that outside air can be manifolded in to fill the need. It figures, then, that any time a combustion heater is operating in your greenhouse, you must provide an entrance for fresh air, even in the coldest weather ...or, I should say, *especially* in the coldest weather.

In a tightly-closed greenhouse with an inside heater, good combustion becomes an impossibility. Poor efficiency will result and, more importantly, the plants will suffer.

BITE THE BULLET AND PROVIDE A FRESH AIR SOURCE FOR INSIDE COMBUSTION HEATERS.

[Area required for a fresh air supply vent for inside heaters should be calculated at one square inch per 2,500 btu/hr capacity of the heater. (Nelson,1981)] This warning, of course, does not apply to electric or steam heat, or if your greenhouse is only loosely sealed.

Back to our situation: Read Section 9 on setting spikes to gauge when to bring the plants back inside. All right, let's take a look at the least understood aspect of phal culture and try to clear up any misunderstanding over how much water phals really need.

Section 3.3 HUMIDITY CONTROL

PHALS LIKE 50-60% HUMIDITY.

That's nice, because so do we but, unfortunately, it's hard to maintain that level of humidity year round either in the greenhouse or in the home.

In the greenhouse, nothing beats an automatic humidity system, period. This is particularly true if you live in a dry climate. You can get by without one elsewhere, probably, but you must remind yourself to check to see if the plants are drying out. If you are good with your hands, you can make your own for about US$100-$125 (1990) or so to meet the humidity needs for a 9x12 greenhouse or enclosed growing area.

Here, in semi-desert, I keep the greenhouse settings at 55% relative humidity during the summer and 45% during the winter. The higher-humidity setting in the summer makes the plants more comfortable and helps to cool the greenhouse. For growers elsewhere, the problem only arises when homes or greenhouses are heated in the winter. In warm climates, you have it wired.

IN THE HOME, HUMIDITY CAN BE MAINTAINED BY PUTTING YOUR PLANTS ON AN INCH OR TWO OF GRAVEL

in a shallow tray or pie plate. Keep the gravel wet. A piece of wire mesh will keep the bottom of the pot up out of the wet. The water evaporating around the plant will provide it with all the humidity it needs. A piece of 'egg crate' plastic diffuser used on some fluorescent light fixtures will work as well or better.

Replenish the water as it evaporates, particularly if heating or cooling systems are running. The problem of low humidity is a serious one in cold climates where low ambient humidity and furnace operation combine to drive levels down under 10% relative humidity. A smidge of Kocide 101 or a few drops of household disinfectant, such as

Lysol, will prevent the formation of algae in the tray. It will also discourage fungi and bacteria.

If you have an evaporative cooler in your greenhouse or home, you'll be doubly blessed. The familiar 'swamp cooler' not only cools the air, but also increases the humidity...a circumstance for which both people and plants can be grateful. Healthier for people, too.

The answer to too much humidity is an increase in air movement and ventilation. Anytime the relative humidity exceeds 80% in your growing area, the time has come to step up the ventilation and air circulation by opening more vents and increasing fan speed or adding an additional fan, especially at night.

Section 3.4 WATERING

PHALS DO NOT LIKE DRY ROOTS.

For that reason, they don't do well as a rule on slabs in cultivation. Unless you are prepared to water at least once each day, more often in the dry weather, stick to growing your phals in pots. I know, I know, they grow on slabs in nature, but the humidity there is 80 to 100% and it rains every day, too...not to mention that most phals in the wild situation die. The ones we know of are the survivors.

How often to water?

IF YOU ARE A BEGINNER AT GROWING PHALAENOPSIS, TRY THIS:

Put a dry wash cloth in a pot similar to the kind your phals are in...and heft it. Light, isn't it? Now, saturate the wash cloth and, without wringing, put it back in the pot and heft it again. See the difference in weight?

Finally, wring out the wash cloth and put it back in the pot and heft it one last time. Relate the differences to a dry pot, a newly watered one and a damp one. Somewhere between damp and dry is where it needs to be re-watered.

THIS HAND HEFTING IS PROBABLY THE MOST ACCURATE MEANS YOU'LL HAVE OF DETERMINING IF A PHALAENOPSIS PLANT NEEDS WATER.

Keep track for a month or two of how often you're watering and develop a schedule from there. After just a little experience, when to water ceases to be a problem and becomes a routine...but even then it is well to heft a pot or two, now and then, just to check. (It also looks very, very professional.) It is true that newly repotted plants are lighter than those that have been potted several months or more. The older the bark is, the more water it will hold.

You are going to find that plants in different parts of your growing area dry out at different rates. Tailor your watering to their needs and the peculiarities of your growing area.

One more time: **DO NOT ALLOW PHALAENOPSIS ROOTS TO DRY OUT.**

Well-meaning cattleya growers have long advocated drying phal roots out before re-watering, just like with cattleyas. Don't you believe it! Look at an established Phalaenopsis plant that has roots growing outside the pot and see how much better the inside roots look compared with the outside ones, assuming the medium is healthy.

One of the least-understood processes that take place when the plant's roots dry out is that of an increase in the salinity of the water in contact with them. There are salts in all but the purest water and fertilizers make the problem worse. As the water dries, the amount of salt in the solution in contact with the root stays constant and the water content goes down.

Result? Increased salinity and, if it gets strong enough, water will start to leave the roots to migrate to the salt! You don't want your root water migrating, do you? Keep your water at home by keeping your roots damp.

ONE WAY OF SETTLING ON HOW OFTEN TO WATER

is to use pots with extra drainage holes or make some extra ones with a soldering iron. Then you can water to your heart's content and not worry about over-watering... because the added drainage will reduce the probability of soggy medium to almost nil. It's like having soggy bark insurance, a very nice thing to have.

It also keeps roots healthier by allowing air to circulate more freely in the pot. Believe it or not, the roots of your plants have to breathe. That's not an easy concept to grasp because we don't normally think of things breathing through their feet, but it's true. Come to think of it, people's feet have to breathe, too, or they get athlete's foot, a fungal disease. Good analogy. If you don't want your plants to get athlete's foot, keep your drain holes open and your bark unsoggy. (I can't believe I just said that.)

WITH THE EXTRA DRAINAGE, YOU CAN USE SEEDLING POTTING MIX ON PLANTS IN UP TO 4-INCH POTS.

That's flowering size on most phals. The plants will grow faster because the finer bark 'conditions' faster and will hold more water and nutrients than does the standard potting size bark mix. It is true that more frequent re-potting is necessary...like every 6 to 12 months, but wait till you see how much better they grow in the finer mix.

Water early in the day and not at all if you think the leaves and, more importantly, the crowns won't dry out before nightfall. When you must water and you don't think things will dry before night, spray the crowns (the juncture of the leaves) with a disinfectant such as Physan 20 after watering to prevent crown rot problems.

I do not subscribe to the idea of putting Physan in fertilizer water for regular application. It sounds good, but there is a compound similar to a wetting agent in Physan that can break down bark very quickly if used on a regular basis. It causes the bark to swell and favors microbial decomposition when the Physan is stopped. Use it on the initial soaking of the bark... or any other medium you may be using...but not regularly. You also run the risk of promoting other problems as well. There have been reports of toxicity in smaller plants from extended, regular use of Physan.

WATER USED ON PHALS SHOULD NOT BE ANY COOLER THAN 60° F., especially when the plants are in spike. The cold water can cause bud drop and some phal flower spikes will wilt and collapse if splashed with water cooler than 60°. P.

pulchra is one species that is sensitive to cold water and may pass the sensitivity on to its progeny. Some phals are hardier than others, but why take the chance?

Solutions to this problem range from using hot water from a gas, electric or solar water heater to allowing water in a container to stabilize at room temperature before use.

One neat solution used by the head grower at Stewarts Orchids is worth noting. Ricardo Mendez bored out the concentrate passage of a Hozon siphon mixer-proportioner to 1/8th of an inch and uses the modified device to siphon hot water from a bucket. When added to the cold water mainstream, the siphoned hot water raises the discharge temperature to an acceptable level. Slick. He only used that technique in Stewart's stud house where it really counts.

I have hot water in my greenhouse from a solar water heater tank in the garage and it's connected to a 2-faucet laundry fixture. I mix a little hot water with the cold before it gets to the Syphonex which is located in mid-hose. I open the hot water faucet just enough to raise the discharge water temperature to 65° or so. It doesn't take much.

I've also seen a shower hot-cold water mixing valve used to temper cold water with a little hot. This is the top-of-the-line solution to the cold water problem.

OVERHEAD, AUTOMATIC WATERING SYSTEMS.

There is much to recommend automatic, overhead watering systems, even for hobbyist greenhouses. The most obvious benefit, of course, is that the plants get watered whether or not you remember to do it or not or when you're busy doing something else such as when you're away working or vacationing; reasons to suit *you*.

There are also reasons why the *plants* prefer a steady drizzle for half an hour instead of a deluge for 2 seconds, the usual thing we all do.

Slow, misty overhead watering soaks potting media more thoroughly than hand-watering does. Intervals between waterings can be lengthened a little and the plants are happier because the wet-dry extremes are tempered. Drizzle-watering also more closely approximates the natural conditions the plants experience and water stress is reduced.

In a heated greenhouse, the fine spray from the watering heads will absorb some of the heat from the air and arrive at the plant in a slightly warmer condition...like warm rain.

Plants on slabs, if you have any, will be much happier with this arrangement, but they still are going to need more frequent watering than those in pots.

On the negative side of the overhead drizzle watering is the probability the potting media will break down faster. If the system comes on and waters during cool, damp conditions while you are away, a Pseudomonas problem could develop. (We'll talk about this in the section on fungi and bacteria.) I've had that happen even when I was at home because, since the timer had taken over responsibility for watering, I stopped worrying about when it should be done.

But, timers do a lousy job of deciding whether watering is or is not in the best interest of the plants at any given time.

If you use this method of watering, you can inject fertilizer directly into the stream of water going out through the overhead system by the use of an injector-feeder such as the Merit Commander. Another worry turned over to a micro-chip.

If you choose to use an injector that uses an electric pump, Lawn Genie makes a lawn sprinkler controller that operates a relay for use with a pump.

Save yourself a lot of grief and use the hard PVC plastic pipe for the distribution system. The flexible plastic tubing is nothing but trouble.

There are other negative aspects of automatic watering, too, like uneven distribution of the sprinkled water. Some plants may go dry. Sprinkler heads may clog and again plants go dry because, with you letting the micro-chip do the worrying, they don't get looked at as often.

If you want to use a system like this, see the schematic diagram. The system is easy and relatively cheap to make with lawn sprinker parts available from many hardware stores or nursery supply houses.

The Merit Commander injector, if you choose to use one, is usually not available locally. I tried for 2 years to figure a way to buy one at wholesale. Although I hated to, I finally conceded defeat and paid the retail price for one. Damn, I hate to pay the retail price for anything!

Some people will disagree with the use of these automated systems for their plants because they take the grower away from close contact with his or her plants. I agree with that premise, but, being retired, I also have a hell of a lot more time to spend with my plants than someone who has to work for a living.

As is so often the case, tailor your systems to meet your personal requirements.

FOR BEST RESULTS IN GROWING PHALS, THE pH OF THE WATER USED SHOULD BE ADJUSTED TO FROM 5.5 TO 6.5, moderately acidic. More on that subject in Section 4 on Water and Water Quality.

Section 3.5 FERTILIZERS

PHALS IN FIR BARK DO WELL ON APPLICATIONS OF A BALANCED FERTILIZER SUCH AS 18-18-18 OR 20-20-20

for most of the year. They need a little more nitrogen for 6 to 8 weeks after repotting, but the balanced fertilizer is an all-round good choice for most growers. With annual repotting, I'm not sure there is any need to use different fertilizers with the various potting media.

I usually use Peters fertilizers, but there are others, probably equally good and possibly cheaper, too. My phals and I find little difference among them. All good.

A point to keep in mind if you are using de-ionized or reverse osmosis water, most commercial fertilizers don't have calcium in their mixes. You'll have to add that separately ...and maybe magnesium, too. Since most tap water has an abundance of calcium, the easiest way to provide it to the plants is to water with

the tap water every 3rd or 4th watering. An alternative to this method is to fertilize with calcium nitrate, but DO NOT add calcium nitrate to any solution that has phosphorus in it; the result is rock.

Calcium nitrate can be applied alone or with ammonium sulfate in a ratio of two parts the nitrate to one part of the sulfate.

I've heard recommendations for use of a 3-1-2 fertilizer ratio for orchids grown in fir bark, but my own experience with phals in fir bark has been better with a balanced ratio. Too much nitrogen encourages soft growth and can cause more rapid breakdown of the potting medium where fir bark is used. I believe it is wiser to use less nitrogen in the fertilizer and condition the water to make more of it available to the plant. I'm pretty sure that is an over-simplification of a very complex relationship, but it is a relatively safe course.

IN MANY PARTS OF THE WORLD, THE pH OF TAP WATER IS WELL ABOVE NEUTRAL AND THE SIMPLE ADDITION OF AN ACID TO THE FERTILIZER MIX WILL PRODUCE ASTONISHING IMPROVEMENT IN PLANT GROWTH.

Conditioning the water is done by adjusting the pH to about 5.5 to 6.5. See Figure 1 for the rationale of this conclusion. Instructions for conditioning water are in Section 4. In any event, start with a balanced fertilizer and conditioned (slightly acidic) water and you won't go far wrong.

PLANTS NEED A HIGH NITROGEN FERTILIZER FOR 6 TO 8 WEEKS AFTER REPOTTING.

Repotting seems to cause a burst of growth.in a healthy plant at any time of the year except during flowering and flower induction. I find I get best results feeding with a high-nitrogen fertilizer during the times when the plants are growing rapidly and a high phosphorous fertilizer during spike and flower formation.

A handy clue to when the plant is actively growing is to note the color of the root tips. If some have green showing and have not 'silvered' over with velamen, chances are good that the plant is in a period of rapid growth and needs the balanced formula fertilizer which has more nitrogen than does the high phosphorous mix.

I use the high-phos fertilizer during spike formation without regard to the growth rate of the plants. Phals grow throughout the year (Batchelor, 1983), but not at a constant rate. Rate of growth is influenced by light intensity, day length, temperature and other factors.

NEVER APPLY FERTILIZER SOLUTION TO A DRY PLANT.

If the plant appears dry or feels light to the heft, water it and put off fertilizing until the following day. Fertilizing a dry plant is like feeding a big meal to a man dying of thirst. It will probably do more harm than good. Relieve the water stress first, then feed it later.

Seedlings require a different fertilizer program from mature plants. See Section 10.

You might also spray the roots with Physan during repotting and to prevent infection through damaged roots. The alternative is to dry the plant out for a week or two, but, personally, I like to eat regularly and I assume the plant does, too.

The plant's need for fertilizer is well-documented, but just how *much* is needed is less well understood. "...limitation of the supply of nitrogen, provided the plant is otherwise well-nourished, tends toward earlier flowering, at least in some species, and an excess of nitrogen fertilizer may retard flowering." (Rickett,1957)

I hate to have to ask you to play scientist to enjoy your orchids, but this issue is very important and even casual growers need to have a handle on the degree of alkalinity of their water.

High pH's are a lot more common than neutral or even low pH's but generally in mountainous areas the pH will be high. This is true worldwide. The same is also true in drier areas. In areas of frequent rainfall, salts are leached out of the soil that ground water passes through and the pH will drop to near neutral or below. Tap water on most of the east coast of the US is near neutral.

In fact, there is a question in the parlor game Trivial Pursuit which asks which of the major cities in the US has the best quality metropolitan water. Believe it or not...New York City. I'm envious, but I like the desert.

If a grower is to err in the use of fertilizer, it is better to use too little than too much. Phals grow in nature with almost none. True, specimens collected in the wild are usually pretty sorry sights, compared to those in culture, but leanness is a survival quality, so go with light feedings and,

WHEN IN DOUBT, DON'T...OR DO WITH LESS.

This is one of the bases of the Principle of Benign Neglect, one of the more successful orchid cultural techniques.

Another consideration is that too much nitrogen encourages rapid, soft growth which is more subject to bacterial and fungal infection. Lean and mean is the name of the game.

If you can handle just one more point:

AVOID FERTILIZERS WHICH HAVE NITROGEN WHOSE SOURCE IS UREA.

By the time urea has broken down into a form usable by the plant, it has been flushed out of the pot and only makes the weeds in your greenhouse grow faster.

Even in soil, where urea is best suited, only two-thirds of urea applied will break down to useful form in 12 months. Nitrate and ammoniacal nitrogen are better for phals, particularly if you have water with a pH above 7.0.

A RATIO OF TWO-THIRDS NITRATE NITROGEN TO ONE-THIRD AMMONI-ACAL NITROGEN SOURCE IS GOOD FOR PHALS.

The plants can use more of the nitrogen from an ammoniacal source when available light is good, so a little sulfate of ammonia can be added to whatever fertilizer you are using to accelerate growth rate. If you can't find the urea-less material, try adding a half-cup of sulfate of ammonia per 100 gallons to the fertilizer solution. This will lower the pH of your fertilizer some. Measure it if in doubt.

A high bicarbonate reading on your water analysis report is cause for using a ratio greater than the usual 2 to 1 of nitrate nitrogen source to ammoniacal. Try 40 to 45% ammoniacal if your bicarbonate count is in the range of 2 to 4 meq/L. Acid treat the water if the bicarbonates are over 4.

Do not use sulfate of ammonia when the light is not good. It will produce rapid, soft growth. Do not use more than the recommended amount because overuse can cause toxicity.

Sulfate of ammonia is used to green-up lawns and is available at garden shops everywhere.

Peters Peat-Lite Special 20-10-20 has the characteristics we've been talking about here and is a good choice for phals. I have excellent results with it. There probably are others of a similar formulation.

Dyna-Grow fertilizers available in the US are also in this urea-less category. It is in liquid form so is easy to use in small quantities, but it is also considerably more expensive than the granulated Peters. Users locally seem to be very satisfied with it.

Every now and again, someone comes up with a new 'miracle' fertilizer, hormone additive, potting medium, or some other golden bullet that will produce miracles, but before you jump on the bandwagon, let someone else do the experimenting...and suffer the damage and expense that goes with new ideas and materials. Don't be anxious to try new things because the plant's needs are quite simple, but if you are one that just has to be at the cutting edge, take it easy and do only a few plants, the ones you can do without.

When I was a kid, a Rite of Passage for young males was to drive fast along a country road on a dark night and turn off the car headlights for a few seconds. That's one of the things I don't do much anymore...just like chugalugging. Somewhere along the line, I learned the painful lesson about taking chances just because everyone else was doing it.

Trendy techniques and materials for growing phals are great topics for cocktail party/society meeting chatter, but they detract the grower's attention from the solid basics of culture. Stick to the basics...unless, of course, glitzy talk is where your interest is. There are no golden bullets, no magic potions, no fabulous elixirs...although it's fun to believe in magic.

If you want a simple formula for success with phals, here's one: There isn't just one magic bullet for phals, there are five; five things to concern yourself with; control of light, control of temperature, control of water and fertilizer, control of potting materials and control of air movement. That's it.

See, I told you it was easy.

Section 3.6 AIR MOVEMENT

Moving air around Phalaenopsis plants is necessary to:

1. KEEP DOWN TEMPERATURES OF LEAF SURFACES WARMED BY THE SUN.

2. PROVIDE A CONTINUOUS SUPPLY OF CARBON DIOXIDE USED BY THE PLANT FOR GROWTH.

3. TO DRY LEAF SURFACES, CROWNS IN PARTICULAR, TO DISCOURAGE BACTERIAL AND FUNGAL INFECTIONS, BOTH OF WHICH ARE ENCOURAGED BY STANDING WATER.

Although horizontal fan systems are common, particularly in large greenhouses, those which move air vertically are more efficient from an energy-use standpoint and also from the perspective of plant health. Vertical fans stir the closed air systems in a greenhouse and prevent layering of air at different temperatures. (I like John Watkins' term, 'homogenizing' the air.) They also tend to warm and cool a house more uniformly and dampen temperature extremes, a process favorable to good plant growth and efficient use of heating and cooling energy.

Plant growth slows when ambient temperatures approach minimums and maximums, so moderating leaf temperature tends to keep the growth process continuous rather than intermittent. With the use of vertical fans, cold and hot spots are eliminated, or at least reduced, and humidity is distributed more evenly in the house. Algae, fungus and rot under benches are held to a minimum, more so than with a horizontal system. However, a vertical fan system does not lend itself well to a large greenhouse and is more at home only in a smaller hobbyist-sized greenhouse.

Vertical air movement is easiest to provide in greenhouses whose height is at least 10 or 11 feet. If you are building, or plan to build, consider that temperature and humidity control is easier to achieve with larger structure volume, read: a higher roof.

Larger volume houses warm and cool slower and subject plants to less stress in the process. Higher ceilings also give you room to use a larger fan.

Pad-and-fan systems work best for larger greenhouses and are in common use. The very large greenhouses don't need fans to move air because convection currents occur naturally in the larger volumes.

Speaking of fans, avoid the busy, noisy little fans of 24 inches or less in diameter. They upset the tranquility of an orchid house, bump your knees (some of them), and burn out regularly (most of them).

The larger 'turbulator' fans in the 24-to 30-inch range are better, but their high (1750 RPM) speeds produce noise and vibration unwarranted and unwanted and, I don't know about you, but I like it quiet when I'm enjoying my flowers. I don't even bother going into the greenhouse when the grandkids are around...much as I'd like to. (I tend to agree with the philosopher who said grandparents are twice-blessed when the little ones come to visit; first, when they arrive and, second, when they leave.)

Slow-moving ceiling fans made for home use are nearly ideal for our purposes. They are readily available (try finding a turbulator in your local hardware store), relatively cheap (frequently on special sales), efficient in operation, move large masses of air at slow speed...and are blissfully quiet.

A 52-inch fan at top speed moves upward of 10,000 cubic feet of air per minute (advertised), more than enough for a 16x25 foot greenhouse. Run it on low or medium speed and it will outlast the family car.

The greenhouse vertical fan should move the column of air *upward*. A downward blast will dry out plants beneath it quickly and cause a watering problem. For this reason, select a fan which offers an up or down option. The option in house ceiling fans costs only a couple of dollars and is well worth it.

If the ceiling fan you use in your growing area has wooden blades... and most do...treat them with a water-proofing compound to keep the plies from separating. It's called delamination and it can be dangerous as I found when a blade separated from the fan and went through the side of my greenhouse.

Another note of caution: If you are tall or have a low ceiling in your growing area, get out of the habit of raising your arms, such as when stretching. The blades will do more than clean your nails; it will clean your clock, too.

If you are competent with things electrical, you can reverse the rotation of some ceiling fans by switching the field leads. Some loss of top speed will be noticed in changing a one-direction fan (usually down) to the other direction. Small loss. It's seldom used at top speed anyway.

If you have a fan speed control, turn it to the lowest speed and move a cigarette around in the corners of the greenhouse, increasing the fan speed until some positive movement of the smoke is seen in all parts of the house where plants will be grown. Upward air movement, incidentally, keeps the high plants (the ones who need it most) cool, too.

AIR CIRCULATION IS SELDOM A PROBLEM FOR PLANTS GROWN IN THE HOME WHERE WARM OR COOL AIR SYSTEMS ARE USED.

If you have even as few as one plant in a single location, though, you should have a small, slow-speed fan for circulation of air. An 8-inch 'personal' fan is a good choice and is inexpensive to buy and to run.

On the way home from the nursery when you bought your first plant, stop off at a hardware store and buy one. Aim it over the top of the plants, plug it in and forget about it. When it burns out, go get another one, because phals like most orchids need moving air to stay healthy. In nature they live up in the trees, right? What do you suppose that stuff is that's whistling around them up there, chopped liver?

A problem arises when plants are grouped together: They increase the humidity in their micro-environment to the point where it becomes a threat in the form of bacterial and, maybe, fungal infections. That's when you need a fan.

OK, those are some of the basic considerations of Phalaenopsis culture and they should get you through the good and better levels of competence. There's more, though, lots more, so let's look at what some of the considerations are for best results with Phalaenopsis.

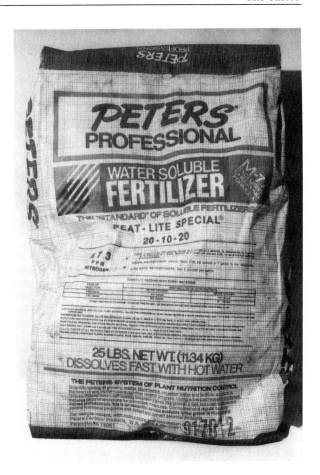

Peters Peat Lite Special fertilizer (20-10-20).

Fresh air inlet...inside view.

Fresh air inlet to heater...outside view.

Ceiling fan in greenhouse.

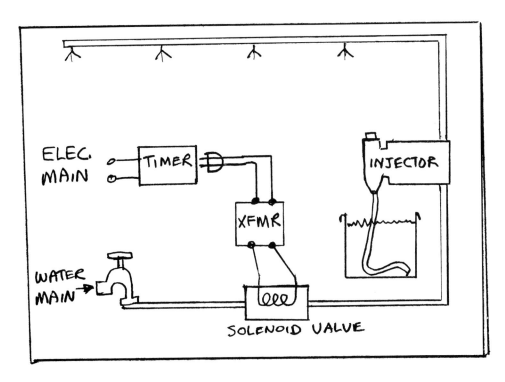

Injector Diagram

Syphonex fertilizer injector.

General Electric T-214 footcandle meter; recommended.

CHAPTER TWO

Best Culture
(For the serious grower)

Section 4. WATER AND WATER QUALITY

Phals respond best to culture when the water which is used to grow, to fertilize and to spray pesticides is...or is conditioned to a slightly-to moderately-acidic state, or a pH of a little less than 7.0. (pH is the term used to describe a degree of acidity or alkalinity, 7.0 being neutral; below 7.0 is acidic and above 7.0 is alkaline.) At higher or lower levels on the pH scale, the various nutrients and trace elements are less available to the roots of the plant. At pH 5.5 TO 6.5 ALL ARE AVAILABLE. This is an oversimplification, but it is essentially correct and enough for our needs here.

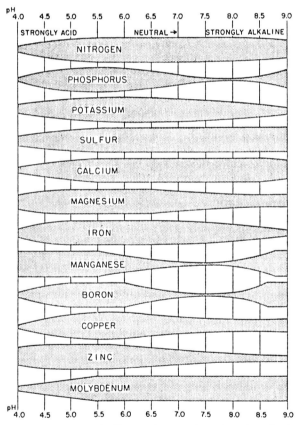

Influence of reaction on availability of plant nutrients (organic soils) (*widest part of bar indicates maximum availability*).

Nutrient Availability (Lucas and Davis)

(Graph courtesy of Michigan State University.)

38

At the risk of losing a lot of readers, I must say that you have to understand a little about the quality of water if you are to become a serious phal grower. It is important to understand what is happening in the relationship of plant and water because water quality enters into almost every process of plant growth. I'll try to cover the minimums here. If you still can't handle it, make friends with someone who can.

Don't feel bad if you don't understand; I know the feeling after running into a requirement for Calculus 101 in an MBA graduate program when I was 35 years out of high school. I never did get a passing grade, so I whined a lot.

WITH SOME EXCEPTIONS, IF YOU DON'T ADJUST THE PH OF YOUR WATER TO THIS IDEAL RANGE, NOT A HELL OF A LOT IS GOING TO HAPPEN TO HARM THE PLANTS.

They just won't grow as well or as fast as they could, given nearly ideal conditions of the preferred pH. I could probably get along OK without a glass of wine or two each day, but I do a whole lot better with one...or two. Same principle.

For best growth then, if you don't already have it,

I RECOMMEND ADJUSTING ALL WATER APPLIED TO PHALAENOPSIS ORCHIDS TO A pH OF BETWEEN 5.5 AND 6.5

or, in words, slightly to moderately acidic. (This rule does not apply in every case to water used to make up pesticide sprays. Read the labels for more specifics.)

In the area where I live and in much of the rest of the world, pH levels of tap water of 7.8 to 8.2 are common. This is in the alkaline direction from neutral, so I use an acid, added to the water, to bring the level down below neutral. (Soda ash or lye is often used to raise the pH of acidic water in swimming pools and spas.)

Any acid will lower the pH, but some may introduce chemicals which are harmful to the plants. I use phosphoric acid because it lowers the pH and adds an element, phosphorus which strengthens and improves flowers and flower spikes. Don't use the reagent grade (85%); it's too expensive.

The technical grade (75%) is almost as concentrated and costs only half as much. Agricultural grade phosphoric acid (0-54-0) is cheaper yet and is recommended, if you can get it. Try a farm supply service.

At the same chemical supply house where you buy the acid, you can pick up pH indicator sticks which can be used to measure acidity levels. (Some growers use swimming pool test kits for this purpose and they are useful for getting a rough approximation, but some only measure the range above neutral. That may be good enough.)

Although meters are available for the purpose, the disposable sticks will do for our needs. There are different ranges, so ask for those which will measure about the neutral point, a pH of 7.0.

Use these to determine the pH of your tap water or call your local water company for the information. (Don't be too surprised if they charge a fee for the information.)

39

Even if you get a water analysis report from your local water company, get the indicator sticks anyway, you'll need them to measure the results of your treatment efforts. If you have an expensive gift coming, ask for a professional pH meter available from greenhouse supply houses such as Geigers in Harleyville, PA, USA; 1-800-443-4437. US$150-200. Hobbyist meters cost about US$50-75.

Unless your water is very salty, it takes very little acid to lower the pH of a large amount of water, so move in small increments. My tap water right now is pH 8.1 and I need less than an ounce of technical grade of phosphoric acid in 85 gallons of water to lower the pH to about 6.2. That's the amount required to treat plants with a Hozon siphon and a 5-gallon bucket of concentrate. Half again as much of the agricultural grade of acid would be needed to do the same job.

The amount of acid needed is going to depend on the amount of salt in your water. More salt, more acid needed. The amount of salt you have in your water is indicated in the water analysis report under the heading of TDS or total dissolved salts. From zero to 480 is considered negligible; 480 to 1,920 is 'increasing' and requires your attention; if it's above 1,920, take up golf.

IF YOUR WATER ANALYSIS INDICATES A HIGH OR MODERATELY HIGH TDS READING, THE SIMPLEST WAY OF COPING IS TO FLUSH OR LEACH YOUR POTS FREQUENTLY... LIKE EVERY SECOND OR THIRD WATERING. The problem is salts which accumulate in the medium or on the pots if you use clay.

AVOID THE USE OF CLAY POTS IF YOU HAVE A SALT PROBLEM WITH YOUR WATER. The salts accumulate readily on the surface of the porous clay and burn roots.

IN MODERATE OR HIGH SALT AREAS, YOU WILL NEED TO WATER MORE FREQUENTLY THAN WOULD OTHER-WISE BE REQUIRED BECAUSE THE ROOTS CANNOT BE ALLOWED TO APPROACH DRYING. (Coastal areas are especially affected where saltwater intrusion into water wells becomes a problem. Use a coarser medium and keep it damp if you are affected.)

When leaching or flushing, use an amount of water equal to the volume of the pot. Allow the plants to drain and dry for an hour...AND REPEAT THE WATERING. The salts are slow to moisten, so a second flush catches them in a state ready to be washed away.

If you have a high sodium reading in your water analysis, i.e. 2.0 meq/L or higher, add some powdered gypsum occasionally to the flush water.

As water evaporates, the salinity of the solution surrounding the rounds increase...and water can be drawn *out* of the roots.

This accumulation of salts on potting media is another reason for annual repotting. If you don't repot on an annual schedule, be aware that you will need to flush pots more often until you do...the accumulated salts.

EVER WONDER WHY PHALS PUT ON A BURST OF GROWTH AFTER THEY'VE BEEN REPOTTED? Clean, unsalty media.

If you have a high bicarbonate reading, i.e. between 2.0-4.0 meq/L, increase the amount of ammoniacal nitrogen in your fertilizer from the usual 35% to some higher figure, but do so in small increments. Toxicity can result from too much ammonia. The cheapest form of ammoniacal nitrogen is the familiar sulfate of ammonia used to green up lawns. If your bicarbonate reading is over 4.0 meq/L, acid treatment of the water is necessary.

As a guide, my local TDS reading is just under 200 and I use about an ounce and a half of agricultural grade phosphoric acid to bring the pH down to about 6.0.

MEASURE THE ACID, DON'T GUESS.

Your water chemistry may be different, so try this as a starter and measure the pH of the solution coming out of the end of the hose. Adjust the amount of acid added as necessary.

Put the acid in a 5-gallon bucket, fill with water and then add the fertilizer. Used with a Syphonex Hozon proportioner at a nominal mix rate of 16:1, that amount of acid will make about 85 gallons of conditioned water.

Water pressure of 65 PSI will give you the 16:1 ratio with a Syphonex. Keep that in mind when mixing fertilizer, too. Lower or higher water pressure will give you a different concentration. If you aren't sure of what you're getting, stick the little hose into a quart (or liter) of water and see how many quarts flow out of the end of the hose before the quart jug is empty. Squirt the outflow into a bucket and measure the number of quarts you have and subtract one. That will give you an idea of the ratio of fertilizer-to-water that your Syphonex and water pressure are providing.

For use with a Merit Commander injector with a ratio of 128:1: In 5 gallons of concentrate, I use 5 ounces (140ml) of technical grade phosphoric (75%) or 8 ounces (225ml) of the agricultural grade.

I know of people who use citric acid and even vinegar for small quantities of treated water. I know it's handy, but don't do it. Don't use any organic acid such as acetic or citric. They can cause phyto-toxicity (plant poisoning) because the form they're in is readily available to feed the micro-organisms in the potting medium...and not the plant. It's like pouring a microbial nutrient solution into your pots. For small quantities of conditioned water, use a few drops of a bathroom water stain remover called Lime-a-way in a gallon of water. It is basically phosphoric acid.

AGAIN, DON'T GUESS AT THE pH LEVEL OR AMOUNT OF ACID OR ALKALI TO BE ADDED TO THE WATER.

If you haven't got indicator sticks or some other means of measuring the pH, don't treat the water until you get them. I know of one passive soul who was adding 3 ounces of acid to 85 gallons of water, locally, because someone told him that was about right for his needs. That's *three times* what was required. That poor fellow is not alone in this practice;

IF YOU HAVEN'T GOT THE NECESSARY EQUIPMENT TO DO IT RIGHT, USE YOUR WATER AS IT IS; better bad breath than no breath at all.

A couple of cautions when using acids:

(1) THESE CONCENTRATED ACIDS ARE BAD ACTORS and should not be used or handled casually. Use protective gloves and glasses when handling and mixing acids with water. Store containers where they won't be kicked or knocked over and mark them plainly as 'HAZARDOUS'.

KEEP ACIDS SAFELY *LOCKED* AWAY FROM CHILDREN; and

(2) if you have a large adjustment to make in the pH of the water you're using on your plants, make it in small increments and over a period of several weeks in order to give the plants time to adjust to the new taste of things. Plants, like people, can get used to almost anything given enough time to adjust. Same idea.

There are several alternatives to adjusting the pH of water used on phals. One is to do nothing...and sometimes that is the best move. Another is to remove *all* the purities and impurities in your water then put back a complete fertilizer, leaving out the stuff your phals don't like.

Reverse osmosis or deionizing systems may be the answer if your local water is really cruddy. Mine isn't, but I just *love* those clean, shiny leaves, so I use a deionizing system. Distilled water is good, but expensive to use on more than just a few plants. If you use any of these alternatives, get a complete fertilizer that has both macro-and micronutrients.

Macronutrients are elements the plants need most of...and micro-nutrients are the trace elements.

The macronutrients include nitrogen, phosphorous, potassium, calcium, magnesium and sulfur. Micronutrients or trace elements include zinc, sulfur, iron, manganese, copper, boron, molybdenum, sodium and chloride.

DO NOT USE SOFTENED WATER!

The salts used to soften water are very harmful to orchids. The calcium is removed and replaced with sodium. Just as with people, a lot of sodium is bad for plants. (Cholesterol hasn't been identified as an orchid problem...yet.)

If you are watering without fertilizing, add acid to plain water in the concentrate bucket, leaving out fertilizer, and go for it.

RAIN WATER IS FINE IF YOU DON'T LIVE IN THE ACID RAIN BELT.

During a talk in Toronto, I casually asked if anyone knew why the price of maple syrup was so high. The answer was quick: Ask your president about acid rain. ZAP!! I asked for it and I got it.

The point is that if your rain is suspected to have anything in it other than rain, don't put it on your plants. Put it this way: If you'd drink it, you can put it on your plants.

For those technically inclined... and the source of much of the tech data here...the state of California publishes a goldmine of information in a pamphlet entitled, 'Water Quality; Its Effects on Ornamental Plants'. I don't remember the price. Write for leaflet 2995 to

Publications, Div of Agriculture and Nat. Res.
University of California
6701 San Pablo Avenue
Oakland, CA 94608-1239 USA

(Ever notice the smallest offices have the longest addresses?...and vice versa. IBM, Armonk, NY.)

Ohio State University recently published a listing of desirable ranges for specific elements in irrigation water. You may find some useful information herein.

Phosphorus (P)	.005	-	5.0 ppm
Potassium (K)	.5	-	10.0 ppm
Calcium (Ca)	40.0	-	120.0 ppm
Magnesium (Mg)	6.0	-	24.0 ppm
Manganese (Mn)	.5	-	2.0 ppm
Iron (Fe)	2.0	-	5.0 ppm
Boron (B)	.2	-	.8 ppm
Copper (Cu)	0	-	.2 ppm
Sulfates (SO_4)	0	-	414.0 ppm
Soluble salts	0	-	1.5 mmhos
Zinc (Zn)	1.0	-	5.0 ppm
Sodium (Na)	0	-	5.0 ppm
Aluminum (Al)	0	-	5.0 ppm
Molybdenum (Mo)	0	-	.02 ppm
Chloride (Cl)	0	-	140.0 ppm
Fluoride (Fl)	0	-	1.0 ppm
Nitrate (NO_3)	0	-	5.0 ppm
Ammonium (NH_4)	undetermined		
Alkalinity	0-100 ppm ($CaCO_3$)		
SAR	0	-	4.0

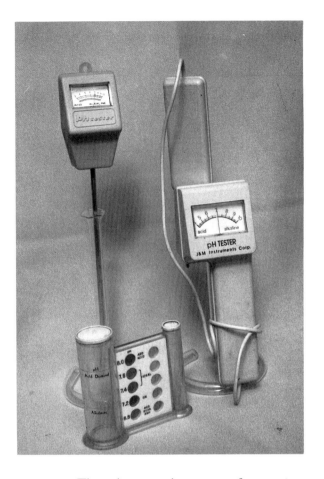

Three inexpensive ways of rough-measuring pH. The gadget on the lower left is a swimming pool 'tester'.

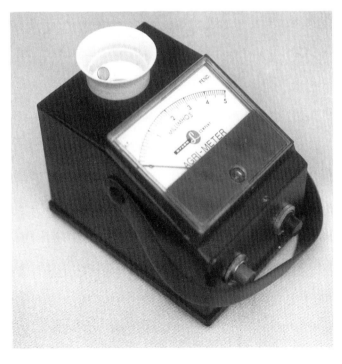

Electrical conductivity meter; measures salts in water. A necessity if you're serious about your phals.

Section 5. POTTING.

If you've potted other orchids, particularly cattleyas or cymbidiums,

YOU'RE GOING TO LOVE POTTING THE PHALAENOPSIS.

It's a piece of cake, a no-sweat operation, and one done mostly in our family by my wife, Nancy, (and our two grandsons, too, as soon as they grow up enough to stop falling over things). It doesn't require bulging muscles, a chain saw and a battering ram as is the case with so many other potting operations like those of cymbidiums. (Ever notice how muscular cymbidium growers are?) Seldom does it take more than 3 minutes to pot a mature Phalaenopsis. So, listen up, you're going to like this.

GENERALLY SPEAKING, MATURE PHALS SHOULD BE REPOTTED EVERY YEAR.

Any phal in a 3-inch pot or under should be potted at least annually or when they outgrow the pot. Over 3-inch may go longer between pottings if the medium is still OK. It usually isn't.

Repot (1) when the medium is broken down; (2) when the plant has outgrown its pot; (3) any time the plant looks less than robust, and (4) just for the hell of it any time you'd like to do something nice for the plant.

Look at the stuff in the pot that's holding the plant up ('medium') and dig down a little and get some between your thumb and forefinger. Pinch it. If it feels firm and resists crumbling, it probably is in fairly good condition. If it crumbles a little, it's in fair condition.

If it smears, it's in bad condition.

If the bark is in good shape, follow the schedule above. If it's only in fair condition, *lengthen* the interval between waterings by 2 days. If it's in bad condition, repot right now.

UP FRONT: June through August ...during summer vacation in the northern hemisphere...is a good time to repot (December through February in the southern) if you want a fixed recommendation. The boost phals get from repotting is added to the already considerable impetus they have toward blooming...coming from lowered temps, increased light and chemical stimulation. Make repotting part of your bloom induction program and you'll see results quicker.

IF YOU DON'T GET YOUR PLANTS REPOTTED BY THE FIRST OF OCTOBER, WAIT TILL AFTER THEY ARE FINISHED BLOOMING.

Section 5.1 POTTING MEDIA.

Choice of potting media or mediums is mostly a matter of price and availability, but keep in mind the media does only two things; it keeps the plant standing upright, and it holds a little moisture for the roots between waterings. That's all it does and many things will fill those simple requirements.

Three criteria for choosing a potting medium are (1) the plant must like it, (2) it must be locally available, and (3) it should be relatively cheap. All of those are important, including the last, because if the stuff is expensive, you may be tempted to slip the repotting...when your plant needs the kind of relief you get with clean underwear. Don't you just *feel* better with a change? Can you do any less for them?

I've seen phals grown well in fir bark, tree fern, rockwool, sand, gravel, charcoal, moss, pumice, man-made porous stone, volcanic rock, ground cork bark, Perlite, styrofoam, redwood products, coconut hair and various combinations thereof. They will even grow in coke bottle caps as one fellow did just to prove a point. (They grow *very* well in discarded wine corks; I know, I have lots of those.)

And each medium has its adherents. I don't bet people anymore that "an orchid won't grow in *that*". One of our local growers manages to keep a few vandas alive planted in fiberglass insulation material, the pink stuff. It's true but, if you want to make your plants happy rather than prove a point, stick with the more conventional stuff.

YOU'LL NEED TWO GRADES OF POTTING MEDIUM; ONE FOR SEEDLINGS AND ONE FOR MATURE PLANTS.

For seedling mix, I use the fine grade of fir bark (1/8 to 1/4 inch) and sphagnum, equal parts, and a little Perlite. These are listed in a descending order of necessity. There is one school that says don't use more than three ingredients in any potting mix. Most commercial growers use only one ingredient, the first. I consider the fir bark and the sphagnum to be a minimum mixture for phal seedlings.

Actually, the "right" mix can probably be

made in a thousand different ways but, if striking off on your own doesn't suit your fancy, try using my mix or just plain fir bark. If you live in a damp climate, leave out the Perlite. It's safe if you use the extra-drainage pots I'm going to recommend in a little bit. I won't vouch for it otherwise.

DON'T ADOPT ANY NEW POTTING MIX UNTIL AFTER IT HAS BEEN IN USE FOR AT LEAST TWO YEARS...BY SOMEONE ELSE.

Let them do the experimenting and suffer the losses that go with any kind of testing. I have not seen a 'new' potting mix introduced in the past 10 years that was one single whit better than straight fir bark or tree fern. I have seen many, many people experimenting and ultimately going back to straight stuff...to the betterment of the plants. The avant garde mix this year does a lot more for the grower than it does for the plants. Makes great conversation and makes the converser sound like he or she *really* knows what happening in the right here and now of Phalaenopsis culture, but that's about all it does.

ORCHIDS WILL GROW IN ALMOST ANYTHING...FOR A WHILE...even pink insulation, gravel or sand.

But, before you become enamored of it, let others use it for a couple of years. If it's still a good idea, try it on a test basis at first. If you go whole-hog on some of these trendy ideas that are supposed to produce marvelous results, you'll find yourself vacillating on things that don't really contribute to your enjoyment of the flower. Don't ask *if* you should change, ask *why* you should change. Ride the good horse until it's proven unreliable.

For mature plants (4- to 6-inch pots), I use the Pathway grade of fir bark. The chunks range from one-half to three-quarters of an inch in diameter. The farther you get away from California, the less likely you are to find it locally, but the more likely to find it at orchid nurseries. It won't come as any surprise that most of the cost of the bark is for transportation.

A 3/8ths inch hardware cloth makes a good sieve to separate the two grades. Use a 1/8th inch hardware cloth sieve to get rid of the fines from the seedling mix. (Use the fines for cymbidium mix or flower beds or trash-can it.)

I use two grades of Perlite in my mixes, small for the seedling mix and large for the mature plant mix.

I hate to say it, but if your growing conditions are much outside the "standard", you'll have to experiment with different ratios and materials in the aggregate until you find one your plants like. If your Phalaenopsis plant roots are fat, white and plentiful, you have the potting medium problem wired. If they aren't, there's something wrong and it could be the medium or the drainage...or both.

Straight fir bark is a good place to start if all these extra precautions don't excite you. Most commercial phal growers on the mainland US use the straight fir bark and nothing else. Too expensive to fool around with exotic mixes and, besides, the phals will do just fine in the straight bark anyway. (I think there's a little self-sufficiency in each of us. "What do you mean, buy spaghetti sauce in a jar? I *always* make my own." Potting media is an area where growers can exercise their individuality...and they do.)

The only variable I can see in the mixes is the amount of Perlite you use, if any, to increase the amount of water held; a little Perlite holds a little water and a lot holds more. Simple.

Good, new fir bark is nut-hard and absorbs very little water at first. However, as it ages and breaks down from microbial action, it holds an increasing amount of moisture. When it's rotten it does a *great* job of holding water...*too* good a job, because then it fills in the air spaces in the medium and denies air to the roots. And they die...followed shortly by the rest of the plant.

Fortunately, during most of its life, the water-holding capacity of fir bark remains fairly constant. If you need a number to work with, most fir bark's useful life for phals is on the order of 18-24 months. But, for the first two months fir bark is used in a phal pot, it can be counted on to hold very little water. After that, though, and through the 18-24 month term, it will give you good service.

Don't plan on using fir bark as a phal potting medium any longer than 24 months. And don't let it go *that* long if it wasn't hard as a nut to start with...which it usually isn't. An 18 month-interval is a disaster if you're trying to do your repotting at a fixed time each year, but it's better than letting things go 6 months past the time for repotting. A lot of roots can go belly-up in that time.

REPOTTING AT TIMES OTHER THAN THE SUMMER CAN INTERFERE WITH THE FLOWER INDUCTION PROCESS.

New Zealand long-strand moss has found a niche in Phalaenopsis culture in recent years. I find it particularly useful for seedlings just out of the flask and for sick plants...but not for use in pots over 3 or 4 inches. You will see some spectacular root growth in the stuff, but it is very, very easy to overwater.

Unless you really have a good handle on phal culture and watch very closely, use either bark or tree fern. If you have any plants in the NZ moss, keep them separated from the rest and water them much less often. I don't think it is a good medium for the casual grower. Just too tricky because, for one thing, much depends on how firmly you pack the damp moss around the roots.

To be on the safe side, soak any kind of moss in Physan for a couple of hours before handling it. Wear a mask if you are handling it dry to keep it out of your lungs. Some mosses are thought to carry fungi which can be harmful to humans.

OK, assemble whatever ingredients you're going to use, dump them in a pile on the driveway or patio, mix with a square-bladed shovel, and put the stuff in a plastic trash can or bucket that has several drain holes in the lowest part.

Into a 5-gallon bucket of scalding hot water pour 5 teaspoons of Physan 20 and 5 teaspoons of either Malathion or Diazinon and dump it evenly and slowly over the mix, cover and wheel the full container out into the full sun. Leave it there for 2 or 3 days...1 day in the summer...and then open and ventilate for a couple of hours and use it. Any wildlife in the barrel that the Physan or the Malathion doesn't get, the 125°F heat will. A dark-colored barrel helps the solar heating. The heating, in turn, kills the bugs and speeds up the 'wetting' of the bark.

I use 5 gallons of Physan solution on 3 cubic feet of bark mix in a 30-gallon plastic trash can. In lieu of the Physan, you can use a fungicide/bactericide solution with a wetting agent (dish washing liquid soap) added. Swimming pool chemicals are used extensively in areas where Physan is not available...or is too expensive. R-D-20 or Naccosan B-60, both American-made, are suitable substitutes.

Note: The use of an insecticide in the bark makes necessary the use of plastic or rubber gloves during potting operations where your hands would come in contact with the medium. Or, you can do as I do and scoop the bark up with a 4-inch pot or a metal scoop. That way your hands don't come in contact with the pesticide.

Malathion is safe enough to be sprayed by helicopter all over the Los Angeles basin in a move to wipe out the Mediterranean fruit fly. I understand it loses its toxicity about 6 hours after mixing. Another reason to use it in the bark you may have to handle.

Keep the lid on the barrel and, if you don't use all the medium in 3 or 4 days, re-wet it before use. Keeping the lid on the barrel helps keep the moisture in and the bark in a damp condition...something the plants will appreciate.

For mature plants, I don't bother sifting the bark or soaking and letting the cruddy stuff sink to the bottom of a barrel of water any longer, because I repot every 12 months. If the bark gets measurably better in the future, I'll think about sifting and going to 24 months between repottings.

When bark in the bottom of the barrel gets down to the fine stuff, I dump it on the flower beds. (The real reason why I quit using horticultural styrofoam to lighten my bark mixes is that when I dumped the remains out on the flower beds, the stryofoam would dry out and blow around...right into the swimming pool. Sometimes you have to think about things other than orchids...that's what Nancy keeps telling me. Sigh.)

ONE OTHER INGREDIENT I ADD TO THE MATURE PLANT MIX IS OLD POTTING MEDIUM, IF IT IS STILL IN GOOD CONDITION.

I can hear some choking at this heresy, but consider, please: The principal problem experienced by newly-potted phals is stress from lack of water. Pre-soaking the bark helps, but the surface tension of new bark isn't broken down completely for several weeks or months after potting, during which time the plant suffers from a lack of water unless you spritz daily and increase frequency of watering to compensate. Most experienced growers will concede the need to spritz, but how often do they themselves do it? For anyone with over 10 plants, probably never.

If you have only half a dozen or so plants to spritz, okay, it's manageable, if you can remember which ones were repotted when. On the other hand, the addition of serviceable, used medium up to 20% of the total volume will "seed" the medium with moisture-holding chunks that will carry the mail until the rest of the stuff is broken in. Right? Why are you looking at me like that, Lady?

I haven't experienced any problems stemming from the re-use of potting medium in the 8 to 10 years I've been doing it. This is due, in part I'm sure, to a 12-month repotting cycle and a conservative approach in deciding whether or not any given batch is re-usable. The use of Physan in the treatment of new bark also helps. If you are really concerned about carrying over bark with bacterial, fungal or virus infections, soak it in a bactericide/fungicide/virucide bath separately before re-use. The principle is good enough to warrant the little extra effort, particularly where bark is expensive...and there are a lot of those places.

Charcoal is supposed to absorb toxins the plant gives off and that might contaminate the medium. It lasts longer than most media and it is also much more expensive. I don't really think this is necessary in potting mix; in flasking media, perhaps, but not in potting mix. But a lot of people do use it, particularly the Hawaiians...and there are some very good growers in that group. If you move to Hawaii, you can start using charcoal, OK?

Tree fern is a good substitute for fir bark if the bark is not available. It lasts longer, but is a bit of a problem to pot and repot. When you've done both, you won't use the tree fern again unless you have to, but the phals love it.

Different regions seem to have different favorite potting mixes and they all seem to work well in the hands of growers who think a little about what they are doing.

Many Aussies use dried pine bark; some growers in the Washington-British Columbia area use a locally available volcanic pumice; the use of a mix of coarse sphagnum moss and Perlite is widespread around the world; many Brits use a slag-stone that is a by-product of the steel making process or rock wool, a mineral product; and the use of New Zealand long-strand moss is growing, but is not without problems. Growers in the Arizona desert of the US even use dried cactus for slab-mounting plants!

Again, the major criteria for choosing a potting medium are (1) the plants should like it, (2) it should be readily available, and (3) it should be relatively cheap.

Section 5.2 POTTING INTERVALS

CONSIDERATIONS FOR DETERMINING REPOTTING INTERVALS FOR PHALAENOPSIS GROWN IN FIR BARK: FOR BLOOMING-SIZE PLANTS:

If you start with good, hard fir bark and you've made the extra drain holes in the pots (that I'm going to recommend) or use "azalea" style pots—you can probably let mature phals go 18 to 24 months between repottings...but any schedule that isn't divisible by 12 months is of little help, because the plants are on a 12-month growth cycle, and you can't just jump in and repot anywhere in the cycle without some set-back. (Commercial growers usually repot year round, but they have no choice. Remember that I said at the outset you can probably grow better than the commercials can? This is part of the reason why.)

That's a broad statement that doesn't take into account how often you water or how much nitrogen fertilizer (high nitrogen fertilizers accelerate the rate of deterioration) you use or how good a judge you are of "good" fir bark, but

FOR A GOOD POINT OF DEPARTURE, TRY 12 MONTHS

and look at the medium when you repot a dozen plants or so from different parts of your growing area. If it looks good on most of your plants, let it go to 24 months next time, but, if you can avoid it,

***DO NOT REPOT* SPRING BLOOMERS BETWEEN SEPTEMBER AND MAY; OR SUMMER BLOOMERS BETWEEN JANUARY AND AUGUST.**

Summer repotting of spring bloomers often will reduce or stop the second or summer flowering, but if you wait until the summer spikes have died off, the following spring flowering will be set back. If you like to show your plants in the late winter-early spring as most do, repot spring bloomers in June-August. If you think the plant is worthy of an award, cut the summer spikes off and force the plant to save its energy...to be used to improve the next flowering.

One more time in a different frame of reference:

SPRING BLOOMERS:

REPOT JUNE THROUGH AUGUST.

SUMMER BLOOMERS:

REPOT SEPTEMBER THROUGH JANUARY.

If you're using fine or seedling mix, 12 months is about as long as you will want to go, even with improved drainage and good bark.

If your bark is *not* hard and dry when you take it from the bag and/or if you don't have time to make the extra drainage holes in the pots...stick to a 12-month schedule for potting. Better yet, use the bark for mulch around outdoor shrubs and get some decent stuff for the Phalaenopsis. Usually the good stuff is hard to find, so keep the 12-month schedule in mind as a fallback position or plan "B".

Do not use bark which has been previously used for any other purpose...other than covering a tree trunk or potting orchids.

If you can handle a principle instead of a date, you can repot whenever new roots are growing...as indicated by their green tips.

FOR SEEDLINGS:

Repot any time they outgrow their pots, but don't leave plants in seedling mix or in New Zealand moss any longer than 12 months. If they're healthy, get them into mature bark mix.

Section 5.3 HOW TO REPOT.

Phals love to be repotted. If you pot them during the recommended times, they will show their gratitude by putting on a dazzling burst of growth in the month or two afterward. (But, keep in mind they need extra nitrogen to fuel the burst for the 2 or 3 months after repotting. See Section 3.5 on post-potting fertilizers.)

Phals are not one of the orchids that like to be left undisturbed for years. It's a bit awkward to repot some of the grande dames like big whites and pinks, mature giganteas and violaceas, but they will be just as grateful as the youngsters for the refreshing change.

Squeeze the pot to loosen the medium and, after removing the plant from its old pot, gently poke away the medium left. Spray the whole root system with Physan. It cleanses, makes roots slippery and easier to untangle and prevents infection at those points where you will cut or break them. Physan also softens stiff roots and reduces the likelihood of their breaking. (Vanda growers take note.)

Sterilize a pair of small cutting shears in a propane torch flame, an alcohol lamp or by dipping and flaming the blades. Brush contaminated cutting tools with a stiff-bristled brush thoroughly before flaming. There are almost *always* bits of tissue left on cutting tools after use and these can shade a spot from the cleansing action of the flame.

Paint the torch flame over the cutting edge, both sides, for 1 or 2 seconds or until the 'sweat' disappears. I have 24 pairs of cutters for this task, so I'm not constantly stopping to sterilize tools.

USE EACH STERILIZED CUTTER ON ONLY ONE PLANT...AND RE-STERILIZE IT BEFORE RE-USE.

(Attention to this detail of sanitation is the key to maintaining a virus-free collection of orchids. The two most common viruses found in phals are spread by contaminated cutting tools!)

Cut away dead roots and part the living ones to get a good look at the trunk of the plant. Cut off any of the bottom of the trunk that is non-functional. The lower part of the trunk with no good roots usually can be whacked off at this point. Reason? The useless extension will keep you from bottoming the plant in the new pot. You like *your* bottom firmly on the pot before starting, don't you?

Trim off any excess of roots...don't worry, they'll grow back.

Whack them off and fit the plant into a smaller pot than you'd have to use otherwise. Big pots lead to big problems like root rot. Saving extra roots is a common mistake made by beginners.

DON'T USE A POT LARGER THAN IS NECESSARY TO CONTAIN THE PRUNED ROOT BALL.

Best combination: small pot and big root ball. Roots remove water from wet media quickly and slow the rot process. Rotten media leads to rotten roots. Make sense? You bet. Short roots, small pots. Besides, big pots take up more precious bench space. If they tend to fall over when in flower, put a stone on the medium surface to counter-balance. I keep a few around for just that purpose. Steve Pridgen puts stones in the *bottom* of the pots of some of his big plants. Neat.

If you want to grow a specimen plant (a large one), invert a small pot over the bottom center of the big pot and proceed as recommended. Good place to stick all those little clay pots that are otherwise useless.

The width of my hand is just about the same depth as a 6-inch 'azalea' pot, so I use it as a gauge and cut off any roots extending below my fist while holding the plant by its uppermost roots. I can hear some growers sucking in their collective breaths at the prospect of cutting those beautiful, fat, white roots...but, don't worry, they'll grow back quickly.

And there is no evidence to support the idea of extra roots providing any extra benefit to the plants. One report says most nutrition is taken up by that part of the root just behind the growing tip. Some people have trouble getting up their courage to cut their kid's hair for the first time, too. On the other hand, there are some very real problems that are associated with over-potting. Whack 'em off.

To repot the Phalaenopsis, simply hold it in the middle of the pot with the lowest leaf attaching point about one inch below the rim of the pot. Fill in loosely with medium, thumping the pot smartly with the heel of your free hand to settle everything. Press down with your thumbs firmly on the medium around the rim (no potting sticks, please) and re-fill to about one inch from the top.

With seedlings, I put mature bark on the bottom of the pot and seedling mix from there on up. The object is drainage.

Any time a mature plant looks a little dry, I add a layer of seedling mix on top to hold moisture; the depth of the layer depends on how puny the plant is. The seedling mix will be washed down into the coarser mix over a period of time and 'fine tune' the mix to the plant's needs.

After repotting, wash the medium down with a generous flow of water, preferably using an aerator on the faucet or a 200-hole water breaker on the hose, to flush out the fines. Run the water till it comes clean. Mark the repot date on the tag and that's it.

I *do not* let the plants dry out for a few days after repotting as is often recommended. The rationale is to let the damaged roots heal before watering, but I see no damage resulting from not doing it. I think more harm is done by stressing the plant by denying it water.

I *do not* recommend the use of styrofoam "peanuts" in the bottom of the pots to improve drainage. First, they may be phytotoxic and; second, they usually do too good a job, because they displace medium that should be acting as a moisture reservoir. If there's too much medium in the pot, use a smaller pot. Given a pot with plastic peanuts and a brighter than average spot in the greenhouse and you have a desiccated plant. If you want better drainage, put larger chunks of bark in the bottom...if, in fact, any additional drainage is necessary.

I see plastic peanuts used commonly by Hawaiian growers and usually with clay pots. If you have a humid climate (and not all Hawaiians do) you may benefit from use of the peanuts. You will see peanuts used in the dry parts of Hawaii too, but the growers have adapted their culture to them, maybe because they only see other growers who use them.

Use of the peanuts is a marketing tool because the seller can put a small plant in a larger pot and sell it at the larger pot price. The peanuts are usually gotten free.

Use of the peanuts cuts down the amount of stored water you have in reserve in the pot. (Growers in dry climates should use plastic pots and ship the plastic peanuts to their Hawaiian friends.)

Use of the peanuts means more frequent watering and a greater probability of water-stressing the plants. Play it safe. Put bark or tree fern in the whole pot. Use bigger chunks in the bottom if you'd like. That should improve drainage if you are concerned.

With the extra holes I'll recommend, no more drainage should be needed.

Section 5.4 POTS.

It's best to make up community pots, from seedlings right out of the flask, in 4-inch square or 3-inch round pots. Leave the seedlings in the compot until they are 2 to 3 inches across, then go to individual 2 1/4-inch pots. At 6-inch leaf span, go to 4-inch pots. At 12-inch leaf span, go to 6-inch pots. If you have one of those humongous things, go to a 7 1/2-inch pot and that should do it.

On the 6- and 7 1/2 inch pots, use those about 5 inches deep. Don't use the deeper ones.

DON'T USE THE 'STANDARD', 6" BY 7" DEEP, ONE GALLON POTS.

They're too deep, hold too much medium (and water), and that promotes root rot.

DEEP POTS ARE BAD NEWS FOR PHALAENOPSIS.

Did you hear me in the back of the room? Pay attention, this one's on the final exam.

AS THEY COME, MOST POTS ARE NOT SATISFACTORY FOR PHALAENOPSIS CULTURE.

I know, I know, they come from the commercial nurseries that way, but that doesn't make it right. Most 4-inch pots have only four drain holes, about 3/8" by 1/4", and, as often as not, some of those are completely or partially blocked by extruded plastic that got there because the pot-maker's mold was wearing out. (McConkey's, a plastic pot manufacturer in Garden Grove, CA told me those molds cost about $35,000 in 1985 dollars. Is it any wonder they are sometimes used a little beyond their normal service lives?

WE HAVE JUST ADDRESSED THE PRINCIPAL CAUSE OF ROOT ROT IN PHALAENOPSIS CULTURE.

The second most important cultural need phals have, after light, is

GOOD DRAINAGE

You've probably heard the advice that good drainage is essential to good orchid culture so many times you could just barf. Right? Me too. But, dreary as it sounds, it is *true*.

Adequate drainage is probably second only to adequate light as the most-violated principle of good Phalaenopsis culture. Usually if a mature phal won't bloom in the first year of ownership, the reason is lack of light to meet its needs. That's probably true of a lot of orchids, but when a phal poops out in the second or third year,

THE REASON IS ALMOST ALWAYS FAILURE TO PROVIDE THE NECESSARY DRAINAGE AND AERATION OF THE ROOTS.

The 'right' amount of moisture for phal plant's roots is a difficult notion to pin down. When potting medium is new the plant probably needs to be watered often, because new bark and tree fern have low capacities for water retention. (No, Mother, in this case water retention is *not* bad.) That changes as the medium ages and approaches rot.

All right, the other aspect of the drainage problem, in addition to medium, is the pot itself or more specifically, the holes in the bottom of the pot.

Unless they are of the 'extra drainage' or azalea type, they just do not do an adequate job of getting rid of standing water in the pot. They don't have enough or big enough drain holes. Small drain holes clog easily.

The solution to this problem is to clear clogged drainage holes and add new ones where needed. You can drill, saw or punch the extra drains, but the easiest way is with heat.

A 100-WATT SOLDERING IRON WITH A 3/8" DIAMETER COPPER DOES A GOOD JOB FOR BOTH CLEANING OUT CLOGGED HOLES AND MAKING NEW ONES.

A propane torch can be used to zap out films which are obstructing drain holes...but make it a quick shot or your pot will be a puddle of burning plastic. The new, instant-firing, piezo-electric propane torches are handy for this and sterilizing uses and should be a part of every serious orchid grower's tool kit.

I bought Nancy a new soldering iron for Christmas back a few years ago because I didn't want her to hurt herself with a drill trying to make holes. She wasn't too happy with it. She may have been expecting a soldering gun, instead.

I got a little worried about all that toxic smoke drifting around her while she was working...so I bought her a fan for her birthday to blow it away. I have to take good care of her. (Tell her I said that and I'll deny every word!)

PHALS IN A 4-INCH POT SHOULD HAVE ABOUT 1 SQUARE INCH OF DRAINAGE HOLE AREA OR ABOUT EIGHT OR NINE 3/8THS-INCH ROUND HOLES. ('Azalea' pots have this many.)

Six-inch pots should have about 2 square inches of drainage or double that of a 4-inch pot.

To make a square 4 x 3 1/4-inch pot acceptable, use a heavy-duty soldering iron (not a gun) to (1) clean out the partially blocked existing drain holes and (2) burn or melt five more 3/8" holes, equally-spaced, in the bottom of the pot.

Mark and Mike at Orchids of Los Osos use a tapered, variable diameter step drill called 'Unibit' with a battery-powered driver to make holes in pots. Neat. No sudden twisting and bashed knuckles. (I bought one for Nancy for our anniversary.)

NOW YOU HAVE ENOUGH DRAINAGE.

When heating plastic to make or enlarge holes, work next to a fan which will carry away any smoke generated. Fumes from hot plastic can be hazardous to your lungs. Be careful, too, of touching melted plastic. It sticks to skin and can cause nasty burns. Allow pots to cool before stacking them because hot plastic can fuse a stack of pots into a single, solid mass. I've thrown away more than just a few new pots with this affliction.

A simpler way to get enough drainage is to buy 'azalea' pots.

BY USING SHALLOW POTS AND PROVIDING EXTRA DRAINAGE, YOU CAN PROBABLY KISS YOUR ROOT ROT PROBLEMS GOODBYE.

Relatively frequent repottings help, too.

One last item of finesse: a nice, little, domestic white wine is 'right' for potting sessions. Keep it simple, nothing sophisticated. The mood is light and pleasant and so should be the wine...and you can get potted right along with your phals.

Pots suitable for Phalaenopsis use.
Note extra drainage holes in the plastic pots upper left,
upper right and lower right.

Left 'scotch' pot; not suitable. Right 'azalea' pot; suitable.

Proportions of a suitable Phalaenopsis pot...under than high
and extra drainage.

Improving plastic pot drainage.

Section 6. CONTROL OF FUNGI AND BACTERIA.

Though here are only two disease problems you are likely to encounter with phals: The more serious is Bacterial Brown Spot or Pseudomonas cattleyae. (We'll deal with the other problem, fungal Leafspot in a little bit in Section 6.4.)

If the Pseudomonas occurs in the crown of the plant, and it will if water is left to stand there, the situation is serious and could mean the end of the plant. (Pseudomonas occurring here is called crown rot.) If it occurs in a leaf the diseased part can be cut or broken off and the problem is solved. (There is a way to clean up small spots without loss of the leaf. The technique is detailed in Section 12.)

Section 6.1 PSEUDOMONAS.

Pseudomonas "is rather unusual in behavior in humans or in plants. It is primarily a 'water bug' that grows and survives for long periods, almost indefinitely, in any situation of standing water or persistent moisture." (McCorkle, 1971) Does that tell you anything about what must be done to control it?

Pseudomonas can be recognized as wet-appearing, slightly darker green spots on Phalaenopsis leaves and most likely to occur when days get short and water spots can stand on the plants through to the night without drying. When it occurs as crown rot, the first indication comes when the growing leaf rots at its base and separates from the plant.

PSEUDOMONAS IS A BACTERIAL PROBLEM AND CANNOT BE CORRECTED WITH A FUNGICIDE.
That makes sense, doesn't it?

Section 6.2 TREATING PSEUDOMONAS

Pseudomonas can be controlled by copper-based materials. I control it by regular applications of KOCIDE 101, a bactericide which is an up-graded copper compound, similar to the venerable bordeaux mixture. (Although Kocide 101 is labelled as a fungicide, it is also a very powerful bactericide as well. In fact, it is one of the few bactericides available for use with plants. It is also an algicide and is probably better termed a broad-spectrum antiseptic.) While approved for use on ornamental plants, it is not specifically approved for use on orchids. The process of gaining approval for use on orchids is a very expensive one and the quantity used under such a license would not justify the expense.

One application of Kocide 101 will provide considerable residual protection during subsequent waterings for 3 to 4 weeks. The blue deposit left on the plants is a bit unsightly and probably reduces the amount of light reaching leaves for a while, but we can live with that considering its other virtues...which are many.

Apply the Kocide spray after a regular watering rather than when the plants are dry.

NOTE: Do not mix Kocide 101 (or any other copper-based bactericide) with other pesticides prior to use. The effectiveness of the copper compound is reduced and can cause problems for the plant.

NOTE: Water used to mix Kocide 101 into solution should not be treated to reduce pH to the 5.6 to 5.8 as recommended in Section 4. In an alkaline solution (pH above 7.0) copper compounds such as Kocide 101 are slow release in nature...and as such will remain effective for periods of 4-6 weeks. In an acidic solution (pH under 7.0) the copper becomes *fast* release and the plants can absorb it fast enough to poison themselves.

Generally speaking, the lower the pH, the faster the copper will be absorbed. The copper is good in small doses, but rapid release can cause copper poisoning...and that can be harmful to the phals.

A cautious approach to using Kocide or any other copper compound would be to alternate its use with an antibiotic such as Terramycin or Agri-Strep, particularly if growth and flowering appear to be less than you expect. There have been reports of harmful effects stemming from long-term, heavy doses of copper-based bactericides, but I have not had that experience, but I used much less than is usually recommended.

The only damage I've seen done to phals by over-dosing with Kocide, is some collapse of cell walls in flowers when I used a three-times the my-normal dosage directly on the flowers.

AVOID SPRAYING KOCIDE SOLUTION ON NEW, SOFT FLOWER SPIKE TISSUE AND ON NEW BUDS. It is strong medicine and can damage emerging spikes and flowers.

If your tap water is naturally acidic, raise the pH to 7.0 by adding an alkali before using the Kocide.

Conversely, some pesticides such as Benlate are acidic in nature, where Kocide is basic.

Benlate works fine in an acidic solution, but, if combined with the alkaline Kocide, it will almost certainly lose its activity. Same result if Benlate is used in a strongly alkaline (pH over 8.0) solution by itself. The answer here, of course, is to acidify the water used to mix.

Physan 20 also has bactericidal properties and is an effective preventive agent against Psuedomonas. Its protection is not, however, as long-lasting as the Kocide and should be repeated every 2 weeks during the high-liability periods. Note: Neither Kocide nor Physan will completely eliminate the Pseudomonas pathogens from potted plants; they will only reduce the surface populations, and, consequently, the number and severity of infections. Frequent inspection of the plants during the high liability periods is still recommended to detect infections that occur despite preventive measures.

Kocide 101, with all its other virtues, is also a very good algicide, so it will hold down algae on greenhouse glass, walks and gravel. It's good for treatment of water in swamp coolers and pad-and-fan systems, too. Use one-half tablespoon per gallon. Anthracnose was reported in at least one pad-and-fan system and 20-25 plants directly in front of the pad were infected. R_x: With Kocide 101 in the pad water, the Bad Stuff doesn't get past the wet, copper-treated pads.

Should you discover or suspect crown rot, carefully cut away all of the blackened, diseased tissue in the crown with a sterile, sharp blade. It's a bit awkward, because you're digging the rot out of a hole, but do this vigorously...and dig until you get to green, clean tissue. Then spray with Physan 20, a teaspoon per gallon of water. Often as not, this practice will arrest the crown rot.

You aren't out of trouble, yet. See Section 12 for the last step, encouraging a new growth.

The plant you've just cleansed is kaput. That's the way it is with monopodial plants...when the growing point is gone, so is the forward progress of that particular plant. It is finished. Hopefully, it will stay alive long enough to start a new growth from a dormant eye, but its days are numbered. Some turn up their toes in a month or two. Others will hang on for a year or more, even producing flower spikes.

If a plant is relatively strong, you can let it flower and have stem propagations made, but keep in mind that the effort may preclude a keiki from forming. It's a decision to be made on the basis of the plant's vigor. If in doubt, cut the flower spike off and apply keiki paste to an undeveloped node under the next remaining leaf. Cut the spike only after ascertaining that there is a remaining, usable node.

If you can't dig out the necrotic tissue, at least score it lightly with the blade to open diseased tissue to the disinfectant which will not penetrate tissue walls, being only a surface agent. Physan 20 will frequently work, but I've gotten better results with DIFOLITAN diluted with equal parts of water from package consistency. A few drops applied directly to the diseased crown works well if the problem hasn't gone too far.

(Unfortunately, Difolitan is only available currently in 5-gallon containers...at a cost of about $145.)

Subdue also works well used this way although I don't know why. It's a fungicide. Must be a side effect. Kocide is labelled as a fungicide, too.

Ordinary old bathroom-variety Listerine will do if nothing else is handy...yes, the mouth wash. It, like Physan, has only a transient effect, though.

While we're on these home remedies, household Lysol, the red-brown stuff, can also be used at one-third the package recommendation. Use a teaspoon of wetting agent in 2 to 3 gallons of solution.

Some antibiotics are touted to have systemic bactericidal properties. I use one, Terramycin, in combination with a fungicide, Truban. More below.

Agri-Strep is also a plant bactericide and may work to control Pseudomonas, but I've never used it long enough to find out.

Section 6.3 PREVENTING PSEUDOMONAS.

The need to catch Pseudomonas problems early makes a good case for frequent examinations of your plants during periods of damp, cloudy weather and regular use of a bactericide to reduce the number of pathogens present on the plants.

As I mentioned earlier, a spray of Physan after watering on cloudy days or late in any day will help to head off problems. A small hand spray bottle of Physan, diluted one teaspoon to a gallon of water, is handy for spot problems and is one of the most frequently-used tools in my greenhouse.

FAR BETTER YOU SHOULD APPLY MONTHLY DOSES OF KOCIDE 101 OR BORDEAUX MIXTURE, WATER EARLY,

TURN UP THE HEAT AND INCREASE AIR CIRCULATION IF THINGS DON'T LOOK DRY LATE IN THE DAY AND SPOT-APPLY PHYSAN WHERE NEEDED.

It may not seem worth the effort, until the day you lose one of the Good Ones to crown rot, and then...

If you mix fertilizers in a barrel and leave them standing in the greenhouse between waterings (as most of us do), add Physan to the mix at a rate of one teaspoon per gallon of fertilizer concentrate in the barrel to hold down the Pseudomonas population. Better still, try to keep it empty between feedings in high-liability seasons such as wintertime.

In fact, eliminate any standing water in your greenhouse or treat it with Physan on a regular basis. A quick and easy way to eliminate one source of Pseudomonas is to flush your hoses before applying water to your plants. Yes, it can proliferate even there. (McCorkle, McCorkle, 1974).

While you have the sprayer filled with a Physan solution, hit the gravel under the benches, the benches themselves, *and* the potting medium, particularly if the plant is overdue for repotting. Pseudomonas is happy in soil culture (McCorkle, Reilly and O'Dell,1969) and the danger of Pseudomonas problems increases as the potting medium breaks down, so add that to the list of reasons for repotting on time.

While Pseudomonas is active in most climates most of the time, it is most virulent in high humidity. Oddly enough, it is a problem in warm, moist climates in the summer and in dryer climates in the winter. It is most active in greenhouses in the cooler fall and spring weather when greenhouses are closed up to preserve heat.

IF YOU ARE USING OVERHEAD, AUTOMATIC WATERING take note. Any pesticide, including Kocide, is going to be leached off the plants if exposed to frequent overhead, automatic spritzing. Some growers use spritzes several times a day in dry weather to keep things moist. The plants are very fond of this arrangement, but keep in mind the need to re-apply the Kocide more often.

I don't like this arrangement, even if it does duplicate the conditions under which the phals grow in the forest. The frequent sprays each carry a little of the copper down to the roots...where it has no business in being. Kocide is intended as a leaf spray only! Do not drench with Kocide.

So, the answer is to spray the Kocide more frequently, like every 3 weeks instead of every 5.

DO NOT APPLY A HEAVIER DOSE TO COMPENSATE FOR LOSSES WHICH MAY BE CAUSED BY LEACHING FROM OVERHEAD WATERING.

You could cause plant poisoning. I suppose it goes without saying that if you live in a dry area and water more frequently than growers in damp areas, you are going to have to spray the *topical* or surface agents more frequently. Systemics are not affected.

LOWER HUMIDITY AND INCREASED AMOUNTS OF FRESH AIR TEND TO HOLD DOWN PSEUDOMONAS POPULATIONS.

Fifty percent relative humidity is adequate for Phalaenopsis, so turn down the humidity settings in the winter...if such a thing is possible. If not buy Kocide in the 20-pound bag. (Instructions for use on the bag is usually in bags per acre. Not much help. Use the one-half tablespoon I recommend.)

In the home or apartment, rest easy, you're home free: Your humidity will be down because of the heating system's operation. You probably will need wet gravel trays more than ever during the winter.

In Hawaii or similar relatively warm climates, use regular sprays of Kocide or Physan to keep the problem in check...and don't leave your plants out in the rain. Phals are *not* an outdoor plant in culture, not even in Hawaii. (Kocide is not approved for use on orchids in Hawaii and their ag inspectors are tough on this item.)

You think *you* have problems with your phals? Growers on some parts of the Big Island of Hawaii...and to some degree Maui and Oahu...have been experiencing a strong acid rain brought on by sulfur dioxide from eruption of the volcano Kilauea on the south end of the island. (It is called 'vog' or volcanic smog, locally.) The volcano has been active for the past few years and, as a result, air pollution by sulfur dioxide has driven the pH of rain water down to 4.2 and of tap water to 5.2.

Can't you just see a New York City grower who has to contend with a hostile environment just inches away from his window sill plants...pitying those poor wretches on the Big Island who have this acid rain problem. Sure you can.

In New York, like most big cities, just breathing can be hazardous to your health, so imagine what skill and cunning it must take to produce a good phal flowering in that kind of a hostile environment? The good growers are not necessarily in Hawaii, Florida, California, Queensland and the like. If all you need do is nail the plant to a tree and forget it to make it flower, there isn't much challenge. The real growers are those who struggle to make their beauties flourish in the hostile environments of the northern, temperate zones and, especially, in the big cities. My hat is off to you all!

Like me, you may wonder why the Pseudomonas problem doesn't wipe out the natural Phalaenopsis populations. Maybe it's because the plants grow high (mostly) in the trees where plant's hides are tougher from the brighter sunlight, where air circulation is better, where drying is rapid and where the plants are relatively isolated from the soil-borne Pseudomonas pathogens. (McCorkle, Reilly and O'Dell,1969)

Purists may decry the use of chemicals where a specific threat is not known, but there is reason to believe that some fungi present on the plants may weaken them and make penetration by the Pseudomonas bacteria possible. Chemical protection is dedicated to reducing the populations of harmful agents on the surface of the plant. These measures can, and should, be supplemented by the provision of adequate bench space and breathing room for the plants.

ADEQUATE SPACING OF PLANTS IS *THE* BASIC PROTECTION FROM THE SPREAD OF BACTERIAL DISEASE.

61

Disease can spread from one plant to another by contact or by water splashing on an uninfected neighbor. Crowd your plants and you can plan on bacterial problems with phals. Better you should prevent them from happening than trying to correct them.

Thinning out your Phalaenopsis collection is an on-going chore if you have more than just a handful of plants. It is a painful experience, but a necessary one, because it follows that you can give more and better care to a small number of plants than you can to a large number.

You don't have to be in orchids long to visit with someone whose collection has gotten out of control and the greenhouse/growing area is jammed full with a tangle of plants that need repotting and de-scaling. Present company excluded, of course, but some of us cannot bear to let go of the other six divisions of a plant that was mediocre at best, but looked good when we started to grow orchids 5 years ago. Ditto for all the junk we won from the plant opportunity tables and the 'practice plants' given us over the first few years and that, somehow, have survived.

As some have ruefully learned, when it gets past a certain point, the mass seems to have a mind of its own and then only a tornado...or Pseudomonas can clear the benches.

We've all met, too, the guy with two full greenhouses and an insatiable appetite for more. He is easily recognized by his glazed eyes, open checkbook and his talk of building yet another greenhouse...this one after he fills in the swimming pool.

TOO MANY PLANTS TO CARE FOR IS A CULTURAL PROBLEM, TOO, AND REQUIRES A DISCIPLINED CORRECTIVE ACTION JUST AS MUCH AS PESTS OR DISEASES DO.

Give them to an orchid society for the plant opportunity table (tax deductible), have a plant sale, give them to beginners for practice plants, give them to a local college or university that has an ornamental horticulture department (Raymond Burr did...tax writeoff), or, as an absolutely last but necessary alternative, trash-can them. It's like cleaning out your garage; you hate to start, but once you get into the swing of it, you don't want to quit. You will be proud of yourself when you do it. (Somehow, this is all related to early potty training, but I'm not sure how.)

Personally, I don't believe in having any more plants than my wife, Nancy, can take care of.

Get your collection down to manageable size and become a ZPG (Zero Population Growth) advocate. Before you can bring a new plant in, something has to go out. All right, raise your right hand and repeat after me, "I promise..."

I met a man in Japan, years ago, who was a chrysanthemum grower and an expert at that. He had *one* plant. Yes, one, but you should have seen that one! It had only one flower, too, and that was 12 inches across. Have I made my point yet?

INSTEAD OF SEEING HOW MANY YOU CAN DO WITH, SEE HOW MANY YOU CAN DO WITHOUT. Go for quality and not quantity.

Section 6.4 FUNGAL PROBLEMS

It is useful to spray the Phalaenopsis plants regularly, during the time of high threat from Pseudomonas, with a fungicide such as Dithane M45 in addition to the Kocide. This to eradicate the messy Leafspot caused by *Cercospora* fungus. Use the Dithane at the rate of one and one-half tablespoons per gallon. I don't think the Leafspot poses a great hazard to the phals, but it looks like hell and makes people think you're a lousy grower.

Note: FORE and DITHANE M45 are less expensive alternatives to Truban.

Section 6.5 HOW TO CONTROL BOTRYTIS

(This was the topic of a seminar at Orchid Expo '88 in Caloundra, Queensland, Australia in September, 1988. This section is based on part of that discussion. The best small show I've seen, by the way.)

The fungus Botrytis cinerea Pers. occurs most commonly in cool, damp, and low-light conditions in greenhouse culture. It is usually not a problem when ambient relative humidity stays below 65%. For many phal growers keeping humidity in their growing areas below 65% RH is a difficult, and often expensive, task. Fortunately, there are alternatives.

The disease does not harm the plant, but will ruin flowers because the blight cannot be removed from the blooms without scraping. Who among us has not lost an award-winning spray of Phalaenopsis blooms to...the tiny, rotten little beast...Botrytis on one or more blooms? I can recall thinking the last time it happened to me that it was much like the tragedy of having one little spoonful of garbage in a whole barrel of premium wine; all garbage.

Botrytis in its very early stages on blooms can be stopped by spraying the affected flowers (and its neighbors) with a solution of a general purpose antiseptic such as Physan (Consan), R-D-20 or Naccosan B-60, one teaspoon per gallon. A vigorous spray will sometimes remove all trace of the Botrytis. All three agents have nearly identical formulation.

Seminar participants' suggested means to prevent the proliferation of Botrytis included the following:

1. Increase air circulation.
2. Increase greenhouse temp.
3. Use a wetting agent to disperse standing water.
4. Use a systemic fungicide on the plants.
5. Use a bleach or strong contact fungicide spray on persistently wet areas (from eye-level down) in the greenhouse.

Let's look at each of these:

INCREASE AIR CIRCULATION

The quickest and easiest means of Botrytis control is to turn up the air circulation by increasing the speed of fans already in use or adding new ones.

In this situation, the beauty of the large, slow-turning ceiling or 'Casbah' fans can be seen. They are relatively cheap, efficient and move very large quantities of air very quietly. Fans are needed in any Phalaenopsis growing area to move air when nature does not provide. You won't have any problems with the Botrytis spores if they're going by your phals at 30 miles an hour.

Most of these fans have three speeds and normally are used in the low or medium range, saving the high speeds for the high liability times. If one of these honeys makes you happy, you'll be ecstatic with two. During the Botrytis season, better you should have too much air movement than not enough; 30 miles an hour, remember?

If you're heating your growing area, you will find the increase in air movement will lower your heating bill, too. Did that one get your attention? Stirring or 'homogenizing' the air breaks up layering and eliminates hot and cold spots. Same as in your home. Money in the bank. Ask any heating engineer.

Small clip-on fans or ones used to cool your feet during the summer can find year round use here, too. Aim them over the top of the flower spikes, but not by much. When they sway gently in their part of the breeze, you know you're in the right range.

For growers in mild climates who don't heat, the fans may be the only method other than chemical to prevent Botrytis damage. If you are relying on the fan method, it might be a good idea to consider two units or whatever is necessary to give double the normally-needed air movement.

DIRECT THE AIR STREAM UPWARD AWAY FROM THE PLANTS. If the air stream were directed downward, the plants directly below would be dried out before others and suffer as a result.

INCREASE GREENHOUSE TEMP-ERATURE.

If you heat your growing area, a quick and positive (but expensive) means of lowering the relative humidity is to turn up the thermostat. If the high humidity situation is of short-term nature, like when it's sundown and the plants are still wet, this can be a very effective solution to the problem. Long-term, you're going to feel the bite if raising the temp is the only step you take.

A more efficient method might be to combine raising the temperature a little with increasing the air movement. If you maintain the minimum temperature of your growing area at or near 60°F (16°C), the use of moving air alone may chill the plants by lowering the 'apparent' temperature...chill factor. In this case, raise the temperature a few degrees *and* increase air circulation.

If the problem of high humidity arises every night during the winter, an automatic 'set-back' thermostat might be in order. It is not necessary to keep the temperature elevated all night long, so adjust the set-back for 4:00 or 5:00AM and by the time the humidity is back up, the sun will be up and the problem will go away...if it's a sunny day, of course.

It's going to be tough to get the desired control this way along the maritime belt or within 5 miles of the ocean or large lake shoreline, but if added heat along with air movement are combined with the chemical tools we have, it can be done fairly inexpensively. (What the hell, you don't want to leave it all to your kids, do you? Teaches them bad habits. Push that thermostat up!)

USE A WETTING AGENT TO SPEED UP DRYING.

You can speed up the drying process by spraying the plants with a solution of Physan (or generic equivalents) after watering. In this instance, it is the detergent action of the Physan that is going to do the job we want done. It causes 'sheeting' action and more rapid draining of surface water.

A 'spreader-sticker' agent (or detergent) will do the job just as well, but why bother with still another expensive product when one will do both jobs? (Please don't read this as a license to use household detergent for this purpose. It is not a good idea.) Besides, the bactericidal quality of the Physan should almost completely eliminate the *Pseudomonas cattleyae* pathogens that can cause crown rot...for that night, at least.

Caution: Do not overdo this practice. Physan can cause a toxic reaction in orchids if used regularly over an extended time, so should be used only when cool, gloomy weather persists or in similar situations.

USE A SYSTEMIC FUNGICIDE

Because many topical fungicides mar or deface Phalaenopsis blooms, a systemic form is usually preferred for our purposes.

Botrytis spores germinate on the surface of the flower and the damage begins. If a systemic fungicide is present when the process of germination begins, the fungus is killed shortly after it intrudes into the plant's nutritional system and sucks up the poisoned sap. And the process is stopped.

No germination, no black Botrytis spots. A flower which has been treated with a systemic fungicide can be heard to say to the Botrytis spore, "Go ahead, make my day!"

Benlate (Benomyl, Tersan 1991) has long been regarded as the standard controls for Botrytis...and with good reason; it does an excellent job. Ornalin 50WP (Ronilon) is a topical agent, but works very well and is specific for Botrytis. A regular program of application during periods of high liability to Botrytis damage is one of the more positive means of control. Combined with the measures mentioned above and those to follow, these chemical tools should be in every phal grower's bag of tricks.

Some growers spray a fine mist of the Benlate (1 tsp per gal) over the tops of the flowers during the humid, rainy season along the maritime areas.

Although Ornalin is specific for Botrytis, unlike Benlate it is not a systemic agent. So, if you are opposed to the use of systemic, this might be the answer. Whether it is better than Benlate is a matter of opinion. Ornalin is newer. You can tell that by the price.

If the Botrytis is breaking out and you need a fast-acting agent to stop it, Exotherm Termil can work wonders. It's a smoke bomb form that spreads a superfine dust in a confined area. One bomb does a greenhouse of 10,000 cubic feet.

Pay close attention to the need to raise the can up high when it is burning; distribution of the powder may not be complete otherwise.

One grower suggested spraying trees and shrubs around greenhouse or growing areas to cut down on the local populations *before* they get on the plants. Sounds like a couple of good ideas; which brings us to our last category of preventive actions.

SPRAY THE SURROUNDING AREAS

The object is to wipe out the bad stuff before it gets to the plants. Spray on, around and under the benches or staging with household bleach or a strong fungicide such as Kocide 101. Kocide is strongly recommended in this regard because it is very effective on bacteria and fungi, is persistent (lasts from 4 to 6 weeks per application), and last, but certainly not least, it's cheap.

More: Sprinkle Kocide 101 on walkways in the greenhouse and it will eliminate slippery algae for the same 4-6 weeks. If that isn't enough, it also discourages slugs and snails. They don't like the copper.

While any one of these recommended measures might solve one grower's problem with Botrytis, a sound program of disease control would include all five. Moving to the California desert couldn't hurt, either.

I WISH I COULD SAY THOSE ARE THE ONLY DISEASE PROBLEMS PHALS HAVE.

There are other diseases that occur only rarely, but a disturbing problem has arisen in the past few years that has yet to be defined and diagnosed. A problem called, for the lack of a better term, 'microfungus' has been noted throughout the US in the past 4 years. (The term is not appropriate because all fungi are micro-) Symptoms include tan depressions on the leaves indicating tissue collapse. These marks radiate from the junction of the leaves outward toward the tips and are found on both the bottom and top of the leaves.

Marks do not appear immediately on the emergence of new leaves, but, from reports, appear in the summer. Sometimes after the appearance of the marks, the leaves turn yellow and drop off.

In four samples I had tested from Ohio and New Jersey, all four were positive for Cymbidium Mosaic Virus, but others have tested plants with the same symptoms and found them clean of bacteria, fungi and virus...at least the two viruses for which antiserums for detection have been developed and are available readily. (There are as many as *21* other viruses that affect orchids.)

The problem may be a virus other than Odontoglossum ringspot virus or Cymbidium mosaic virus.

At this point, spring 1990, I haven't got a clue, but soaking the plant in a solution of Natriphene seems to arrest the progress of the disease when the plant is soaked *for 24 hours.* John Niedhamer reports one researcher found root rot or Rhizoctonia in plants that had symptoms similar to the 'microfungus'. At this writing, the researcher is testing to see if the problem reponds to Benlate or Terrachlor 75WP, fungicides which are specific for Rhizoctonia and which are relatively inexpensive.

The root rot problem might explain why a fungus has not been cultured from leaf samples...and why drenching rather than a topical spray might be needed to control the disease. Work is under way.

A possible fix is offered in the following commentary by John Miller which appeared originally in *Phalaenopsis Culture: A Worldwide Survey* edited by this author.

"On the basis of 'never marry a spray', for contact sprays we rotate from Dithane 78 to

Difolitan. However, sometimes a condition prevails that is caused by a systemic infection of microfungi. As there are literally hundreds of these, the symptoms vary from plant to plant.

Some of the more common are a spotty, ill-defined chlorosis; a streaky chlorosis beginning at the edge of the leaf where it looks as if the leaf edge had been burned with a match or candle; a red-brown coloration appearing at the apical third or half of the lower leaves followed by a dehydrated and senescent (old) appearance and also mesophyll tissue collapse where deep pitting becomes apparent on the surface of the leaves. This latter condition can also be caused by cold water and by virus infections. However, in the latter instance, the pitting is usually dark-brown to black in appearance rather than the white to light-fawn as caused by fungi. Treatment is as follows:

Day One;

* Ridomil 2E (A bit cheaper than Subdue, but only Subdue is legal for ornamental plants. ed), one teaspoon per five gallons of water and in the same spray mix,

* Bayleton 25% WP four teaspoons per five gallons.

(Spray until it runs down off the leaves. It goes without saying that you should wear breathing mask, gloves and protective clothing for any spraying job.)

Day Two;

* Triforine (Funginex), two teaspoons per gallon

Thirty days later;

* repeat the process.

The reason for the 30-day separation is that Bayleton, if used too strongly or too often, can cause shortening of the flower spikes. (Watch the rate of application. Too high a rate of Bayleton is the same as respraying too soon. ed)

I have used this combination three times for microfungus with good results. The affected leaves will continue to die and improvement will be seen in the new growths. This treatment was developed by my good friend, Don Baker."

The process should be repeated at 6-month intervals for an additional year.

We still don't have a handle on what is causing the disease yet or even what it is, but efforts are underway at two state universities. It may be a fungal disease and virus in combination, confusing the diagnosis, but there is little question that the disease weakens the plant and leaves it susceptible to the more common ailments such as Pseudomonas cattleyae.

Bayleton may be the agent that is correcting the problem, however. There have been reports that the Bayleton alone will correct the problem. There is one report that Subdue alone corrected the problem.

Symptoms of the problem are similar to those of a photo of a specimen of fungal Leafspot caused by Guignardia sp. shown on page 84 of the 1986 edition of the AOS's Handbook on Orchid Pests and Diseases. However, to date, that disease only has been reported in vandas and ascocendas. If the disease is fungal in nature, it does not respond to the standard culture tests. At least three efforts have resulted in no germination.

It is possible the problem is a virus which is not detected by the standard CyMV and ORSV antiserum tests. There are a few others that affect phals and there is always the possibility of a new one.

Don Raum in Boston reported that Miltonias and Angracums may also be affected by the disease...and I've got a Rhyncostylis that looks very suspicious and has tested negative for both CyMV and ORSV.

Stay tuned. When we find something definitive on this matter, maybe we can get the major orchid periodicals to print the story. In the interim, a broad spectrum antiseptic such as Kocide 101 will do much toward keeping down the surface populations of both bacteria and fungi. If you think you have the problem, isolate the plants and try the Natriphene or systemic fungicide treatments.

Kocide 101; an indispensible, broad-spectrum antiseptic which meets almost all phalaenopsis disease-prevention needs.

Phalaenopsis virus-prevention kit: Grain alcohol (cheap), a propane (butane) torch, a stiff-bristled brush...and cutters.

Section 7. ALL YOU REALLY NEED TO KNOW ABOUT VIRUSES:

Viruses are tiny, infectious agents which cause chronic illnesses in plants and animals. (Animals have auto-immune systems to fight off illnesses; plants do not.) Unfortunately, at present, the only way to kill the virus in a plant is to destroy the plant; not exactly a worthwhile alternative.

Sometimes the symptoms of virus are detectable by sight and other times they are not. The only way to tell for sure if your plant has one of the two most common viruses is to have a test done by one of several labs around the country or do it yourself with a home kit made by one of the labs advertising in orchid periodicals. At present there is no way for the hobbyist to tell if his plant has one of the other 21 viruses thought to infect orchids. That's a hell of a note, but that is the way it is right now. The only rational thing we can do until a means of virus identification is available to everyone is to

TREAT ALL YOUR PHALS AS IF THEY WERE VIRUSED AND, AT LEAST, THOSE THAT ARE WILL BE ISOLATED.

Many virused plants show no outward sign of the disease. Some do and, in the hands of some growers, these plants would be tested by one of the various reliable indicators for the presence of cymbidium mosaic virus (CyMV) or odontoglossum ringspot virus (ORSV), the most common ones.

There probably are very few collections of orchids today that are not to some degree infected by viruses. (Batchelor,1982)

While the technology to limit the spread of viruses is available, the likelihood of hobbyists or commercial growers observing the rigid discipline necessary for control...is small. Moreover, if you have a sizeable collection it would seem a bit unrealistic to test all your plants regularly; not only unrealistic, but indeterminate as well, because all the test does is to tell you what the condition of the plant was *at that time*. If it was healthy, there is no guarantee that it will stay that way.

The answer to the virus problem in orchids will not be found in this section. It may not be found in our lifetimes, probably because a solution offers too small an economic incentive to draw the focus of current technology.

It's a pretty sorry admission, but about all we can do is slow down the spread of the viruses and isolate or destroy the more serious cases.

Compounding the problem is the common occurrence of finding both the CyMV and the ORSV in the same sick plant. This is the reason why both tests should be done when a plant is suspected of being diseased.

I don't want to disappoint the purists, but if I have to test each plant in my collection every other year for virus, I'll go back to flying sailplanes for a hobby. I grow orchids because I like flowers, not because I like to play scientist. I know a couple of growers who are obsessed with cleanliness and they aren't much fun to be around. This also has something to do with early toilet training, I think.

At present there is almost no way, (short of an obsessive preoccupation with virus-avoidance) of building and maintaining a virus-free collection. I guess you *could* test everything and throw the virused ones away, but...

Most growers say they would dispose of plants that were known to be virused. Some would isolate and possibly breed with the better ones as pod parents only, a practice which appears to be quite safe if the capsules are allowed to go to full term and the seed shaken out rather than green-podded. But, that isn't the answer, either, because the sterilizing process kills many of the seeds...very often all of them.

BUT THE OBVIOUS QUESTION GOES UNANSWERED.

If virused plants can go undetected, how can you tell the condition of your collection at any given time? I have several thousand plants and little motivation to begin testing all of them. Until we have something like a little pop-up indicator or a button that turns blue when the plant is infected with CyMV or red when infected with ORSV, we just won't have a convenient way of knowing.

Until someone advertises that pop-up indicator or color indicating button for sale, about all we can do is test when the visual clues are there, watch sanitation measures very closely and control aphids, if they are a local problem. What a dismal prospect!

BUT THERE ARE MEASURES WE CAN TAKE TO LIMIT THE SPREAD OF THE DISEASES.

Personally, I find it useful to presume that every plant I handle is virused and act accordingly. That way, if I DO have diseased ones, they are likely to keep their condition to

themselves. I test all the plants I breed with and those I use to make stem propagations. At this time, I do not use virused plants for breeding, but probably will if the right one comes along.

READ THIS CAREFULLY!

An article of considerable interest on the subject of viruses and their means of transmission appeared in the October 1987 issue of the American Orchid Society *Bulletin* and is excerpted here:

* "Cymbidium mosaic virus and odontoglossum ringspot virus, the most common viruses in orchids, are *not transmitted by insects*, but rather by contaminated pruning tools."

* "Decontaminating tools will not only stop CyMV and ORSV, but also the other 20-some viruses that have been identified with orchids."

* "...While transmission studies with orchid viruses per se have been limited, at least six have been shown to have aphid carriers."

* "Aphids are either proven or highly suspect vectors of many orchid viruses and pose a threat even when they are not causing obvious damage to plants through their feeding."

* "It may be many years before the transmission relationships of all orchid viruses are fully resolved, but until then, a careful aphid control program is advised. Controlling aphids and routinely sterilizing pruning tools (household bleach is recommended) when dividing plants or cutting flowers are likely to be very helpful in minimizing the spread of most viruses in greenhouse-grown orchids."[1]

It would seem to be prudent to take preventive measures to keep aphids away from your plants if they are a local pest. Sooty molds are an indication of their presence. Orthene 75S at 1 teaspoon per gallon is a good control. Cygon 2E, Mavrik, Dycarb, Diazinon, Dursban, and Meta-Systox R are also specific for aphids. If you prefer a non-toxic control, Safer Soap is labelled for aphids.

Beside CyMV and ORSV, Cucumber Mosaic Virus (CMV) has also been known to infect phals. One way to reduce your exposure to the CMV is to elimate plants that attract the aphids from your immediate growing area. These include Zinnia, wandering jew, spinach, cowpea and nicotiana.

DETECTION: Some spider mite damage looks much like the popular mental image of virus symptoms. A magnifying glass can clear up any confusion quickly. If the damage is stippled, you're off the hook. I never had problems with mites until I got a magnifying glass.Then all of a sudden, there they were!

Means of detecting viruses include home and lab antisera analysis, electro-and light-microscopy, indicator plants, (all of which are fairly reliable); and the eyeball technique, (which is not). The trouble with visual appraisal is that you only see the worst cases. Viruses may go almost symptomless and undetected in a plant for years.

LACK OF VIGOR OF THE PLANT CHARACTERIZES ALL VIRUSED PLANTS WHETHER OR NOT THE SYMPTOMS ARE DETECTABLE.

Many phal growers I've met are quick to point out that they have no virused plants...but, the same growers also admit they have no means of detecting virus.

Home test kits, such as those produced by Orchis Labs of Burdett, NY, appear to be a realistic means of virus control which starts with identification. The use of Orchis' gel-diffusion technique was recommended by the three research scientists who wrote the above article.

I have used a hobbyist kit produced by AnTec Lab of Ithaca, NY and find it easy to use and, unfortunately, accurate. I wasn't too happy in reading some of the bad news the kit gave me. Bob Wellenstein of AnTec makes what could be a confusing process...a piece of cake.

Another article in the AOS Bulletin, this time in 1986, detailed some common questions and misconceptions concerning orchid viruses... which are of concern to most serious phal growers. I've lifted some of those points here:

* "Although cymbidium mosaic virus (CyMV) and odontoglossum ringspot virus (ORSV) infect most orchids, they rarely, if ever, are transmitted through seed."

* "...it is strongly recommended that orchids to be meristemmed be tested for virus first and only those which are virus-free be processed for tissue culture."

* "Will I transmit virus to my orchids if I smoke cigarettes? No...because tobacco mosaic virus (TMV) does not infect orchids readily. Nevertheless, since TMV does have an exceptionally wide host range, it is advisable for growers who smoke to wash their hands thoroughly (including scrubbing fingernails) or to wear plastic gloves before handling any ornamental plants such as gesneriads, which are very susceptible to TMV."

* "What is effective in sterilizing tools and pots between use? ...Unlike fungal or bacterial organisms which can move in air currents and splashing water, viruses must be moved in leaf sap or plant residue by the grower... Disposable razor blades or several knives/shears which have been soaking in either a 10% household bleach solution, a saturated solution of trisodium phosphate (available in drug stores) or a solution of 2% NaOH (sodium hydroxide) plus 2% formaldehyde are all acceptable."

* "If a grower has a series of tools to be used, excess plant residue should be wiped off before placing in the solution. Position the tools such that the last tool (in) gets reused last. "

DECONTAMINATION: Heat can also be used to disinfect tools and/or pots. Tools can be dipped in alcohol (I use the cheapest vodka I can buy) and flamed, preferably with a propane torch, for several seconds. A simple alcohol dip and short flaming with a match or candle may not create enough heat to inactivate the virus.

Brush contaminated cutting tools with a stiff-bristled brush thoroughly before flaming. There are almost *always* bits of tissue left on cutting tools after use and these can shade a spot from the cleansing action of the flame. Paint the torch flame over the cutting edge, both sides, for 1 or 2 seconds or until the 'sweat' disappears. I have 24 pairs of cutters for this task, so I'm not constantly stopping to sterilize tools.

I do not subscribe to the notion that cutting tools must be heated to a red hot condition to destroy surface pathogens. That's over 1,000 degrees F.! If it takes 1,000 degrees to kill off plant pathogens, we *all* might just as well take up sailplanes. It just is not necessary and, besides, your replacement costs for new cutters will look like your monthly car payment.

* "Although virus particles have been observed in pollinia of virus-infected orchids, unless the receptor plant is actually wounded, there is little chance of infecting it. ...Our studies of seedlings which had been green-podded from one or both infected parents showed that no infected seedlings were produced. Although the chances of transmission are very low, if the mother tissue (placenta) is infected, and wounding of the seedling occurs with transfer of sap from the mother tissue to the seedling, it is possible that transmission could occur, but this appears to be extremely rare.

* "Once any plant is infected with a virus, it and all of its propagative parts are likely to be permanently infected."

* "Should I destroy all my infected plants? As long as an infected orchid continues to bloom, it does not necessarily have to be discarded ... If healthy and virus-infected plants are maintained in close proximity, it is recommended that one *never* work with the infected plants and then move to the healthy ones. It would be wise to not even work with infected orchids the same day as the healthy... If healthy and diseased plants are kept together, special care should be taken to control aphid colonies, which sometimes appear on the inflorescences, in order to control viruses known to be aphid-borne, such as cucumber mosaic virus(CMV)."

* "What is the recommended strategy for control of orchid viruses? The most important consideration is an awareness and demand for a quality product by the orchid grower.

Whenever new orchids are purchased, be suspicious of them and have them tested before you add them to your healthy group."

* "...As long as infected orchids produce enjoyable blooms, they can be maintained, but certainly they should be separated from the healthy ones."

These few paragraphs summarize the virus problem better than anything I've seen to date. It is not a hopeless situation; it can be controlled; and we *can* enjoy them, warts and all. As orchid growers, I think we all owe a debt of gratitude to the five researchers who did this work and these two articles...and also to the AOS *Bulletin* for publishing it.

PREVENTION: There is little chance of harming a virused parent plant by putting unvirused pollen on it...and if pollen from a virused plant is used on an unvirused plant, there appears to be only a rare possibility of infecting the pod parent. Most authorities agree that through dry-podding, the progeny of a virused cross can be protected from the virus because the virus does not bridge the placental fuzz to the seed.

In dry-podding, the seed capsule is allowed to ripen fully and the seed is poured out into a vessel for sterilizing before sowing.

If a cross is desirable enough, the extra effort would seem justified; but, many growers point out that they'd rather use a different, unvirused plant and forget the whole virus problem.

FLAME TOOLS BEFORE USE; ISOLATE SUSPECTED CARRIERS AND HAVE A SAMPLE OF LEAF TISSUE TESTED; AND BITE THE BULLET BY DISPOSING OF THE DISEASED PLANTS.

One further thing you might be careful of: The human thumbnail is probably the worst offender around for spreading orchid virus. If you must use it for plucking off flowers, flame it first.

There is little else to be said of any significance on the subject until we find a way to cure the problem without killing the plant.

Before you dump the sick plants, consider if you'd like to keep them in permanent isolation from the well ones. You can still enjoy them and, if you're very careful, you may be able to breed with them.

Before you make any crosses with a plant known to be virused, consider that you may spend 3 to 5 years raising sick plants. It may not be worth the effort.

An interesting sidelight to this issue is M. Maurice LeCoufle's 'museum' where he keeps virused plants of exceptional worth in the hope of discovery of a means of curing the virus without destroying the plant. The room is isolated from the rest of his greenhouses and visitors are asked to touch nothing in it. On the day I visited that room, there were some lovely things in bloom...that the world may never see and enjoy. (sigh)

(For more information on viral infection in orchids, see Orchid Culture-17-Diseases, Part 3—Victims of Virus. American Orchid Society Bulletin 52(7) 719-727, July 1982).

That's about all I want to say on such a depressing subject. Let's move on to something a bit more cheerful, like bugs.

Endnotes:

1. Zettler, F., G. Wisler, M. Elliot and N. Ko, 1987; Some New Potentially Significant Viruses of Orchids and Their Probable Means of Transmission; *Amer. Orchid Soc. Bull.* 56; 1045-1051

2. Wisler, G., F. Zettler, and T. Sheehan, 1986; Common Questions and Misconceptions Concerning Orchid Viruses; *Amer. Orchid Soc. Bull.* 55:472-479

Section 8. CONTROL OF PESTS

A Phalaenopsis orchid without pests is like a dog without fleas. They've either got them, are just getting rid of them, or are just about to get them.

Now, I don't want to sound pessimistic about pest control, but it is necessary to put things into perspective. You never get rid of them all, you just keep their numbers...and the damage they do... down to manageable level. The military calls that 'damage control'.

And that is a good way of thinking of the problem and to avoid the exasperation that can result from the apparently un-ending tide of the little beasties that seem to come from nowhere. I can't imagine how they found out I had orchids. I swear, I think the little suckers come in like pollen on the wind.

But, our problem is getting rid of them, or at least diverting them to someone else's yard.

PESTS AND BARK. A major source of pests is the fir bark we use, if we use the ordinary, decorative stuff. Pests can make a perfect entrance, camouflaged and all, right in the potting medium. My understanding is that the only difference between 'horticultural' bark and the pathway bark you get at K-Mart is that the former is steam-treated to destroy pests—and there are lots of them that may be riding along. (In some cases, there is no difference, except the label...and the price.) The insecticide that we added to the preliminary bath given to a new batch of potting mix(covered in Section 5) will solve the problem for us very nicely.

A nifty move right up front, one more time:

DRENCH NEW BARK WITH AN INSECTICIDE AND ALLOW TO STAND OVERNIGHT...OR BETTER STILL, ALL DAY IN THE HOT SUN.

I use Malathion for treatment of the bark. I don't use it much anymore as a control spray, but it does a good job of pre-treating bark and has the added advantage of running out of zip about 6 hours after it is mixed...so you don't run the risk of handling toxic stuff when potting. It won't stop slugs and snails, though. For them, sprinkle a little granulated snail bait on the surface of the medium of newly-potted plants. Cookes snail bait is good; Ortho with Mesurol is better. That should stop most of the nasties that come riding in on potting bark, including bush snails which are common in fir bark.

Bush snails are the tiny (1/4 inch), but destructive cousins of the big ones. Even if you use media that do not include fir bark, you might consider the wisdom of a similar up-front preventive measure.

For my uses, Orthene 75S (a soluble powder) does a good job in getting rid of mealybugs and whatever else comes along. On the rare occasion when I see some scale, I treat with Cygon 2E. Wettable or soluble powders are preferred to the liquid emulsions because the hydrocarbon carriers do much of the damage people experience with their plants.

PESTICIDES AND pH. Much has been written on the importance of pH of water used to make up pesticide solutions. With the exception of Kocide 101 and the other coppers which need an alkaline water, most pesticides should be used with water at a pH of about 7.0. The problem is breakdown of the pesticide material at higher pH's.

While the practice of using conditioned water whose pH has been adjusted is not uncommon, spraying pesticides with conditioned water is. Use of neutral pH water for pesticides is recommended by the Calif. Department of Agriculture. (Stegmiller, Hawthorne,1980)

This recommendation is intended to prevent hydrolysis or break-down of some common pesticides, something that occurs once in a while in an alkaline solution. The result is an ineffective pesticide. I'm not clever enough to remember what the results were before I started to use the conditioned water in pesticides, but they certainly are good now.

The 'hydrolysis' referred to here is a process that takes place over hours or days, not instantaneously as you might think. To avoid any problems of this sort, mix the materials when you are ready to use them and get rid of whatever you don't use at that one spraying.

IF YOU'VE WONDERED WHY YOU DON'T ALWAYS GET GOOD RESULTS WITH SOME PESTICIDES, THIS MAY BE THE REASON.

To mix pesticide sprays, I use the same procedure I use to condition fertilizer water, but add pesticide instead of fertilizer.

NOTE: CONDITION THE WATER FIRST, *THEN* ADD THE PESTICIDE. IT *IS* IMPORTANT.

SOME RULES:

1. 68°F IS A GOOD TEMPERATURE TO MIX PESTICIDES. DON'T HEAT THE SOLUTION MORE THAN THAT.

2. DON'T USE ALCOHOL TO DISSOLVE THE PESTICIDE MATERIAL.

3. USE THE SOLUTION IMMEDIATELY. IF NOT USED, DISPOSE OF IT AND MIX NEW STUFF THE NEXT TIME.

APPLICATION. Insect populations adapt and evolve quickly in response to the use of pesticides, so in your 'get 'em good' program,

A BASIC TENET IS ROTATION OF INSECTICIDES.

There are several reasons for rotating pesticides. Not the least of these is to foil any attempt by the bug population to evolve a pesticide-resistant strain of new bugs. Another, certainly, is to use a broad brush so that few of the common pests are overlooked.

Regarding insect resistance and adaptation to pesticides, it's worth remembering that systemic materials usually create resistance problems faster than the non-systemics. Because of the chemistry involved, the systemics usually affect a specific chemical factor in insect metabolism and any insect with an odd metabolism is unaffected. This insect could become a parent of a new strain of insects resistant to the systemic insecticide. The principle above also applies to fungicides. This problem has led to the current practice of combining fungicides to create a broader spectrum of efficiency and knock down those odd populations. Kocide 101 and Dithane M-45 is a common mixture used.

PESTICIDE EXPERTS ADVISE THAT THE SIMPLEST AND MOST EFFECTIVE METHOD OF PEST CONTROL IS TO PREVENT THEIR ENTRY;

this, rather than laboring to eradicate them once they've moved in. Pest management, so to speak.

For example, hold off putting new plant purchases in with your older ones. Quarantine them for a week or two and treat them heavily. Mealybugs, scale and mites often arrive on those new plants.

Most experienced growers advise this, but how many growers do you know that actually do it? The smart ones, that's who.

TURN OFF THE FANS IN YOUR GREENHOUSE BEFORE SPRAYING PESTICIDES. Obvious.

One further caution regarding the use of pesticides: It makes sense to try out a new pesticide on just a few plants, particularly if you're not too clear on the recommended dosage. A friend used a new (to him) pesticide a few years back and used it in accordance with the directions on all his 2-3,000 cattleyas in one treatment. He eventually threw away 42 plastic trash bags (1,000 mature plants) of sick or dead plants, and it was 3 years before the survivors began to grow and bloom again normally. His indiscretion? He used an outdoor pesticide in a greenhouse and assumed liquid Orthene was OK for his whole collection. It wasn't. Don't let that happen to you!

There really aren't many different pests to cope with in Phalaenopsis culture. The most common are mealybugs, mites, soft and hard scale and slugs and snails. In some areas, aphids are a threat. Occasionally, a grasshopper or a mouse will chew up the edges of a few plants, but they're usually not a persistent problem; the others are. That's why

YOU NEED A REGULAR PROGRAM OF APPLICATION OF PEST KILLERS

if you are to avoid sharing your beauties with the hungry legions of them. (Dr. McCorkle, cited earlier, advises that even the seemingly innocuous lizards found scampering about some greenhouses are not so innocuous. Their droppings can cause bacterial problems in orchids.)

The problem is less severe if you grow your phals in the house than it is if you grow them in a greenhouse. The number of the pests seems to rise logarithmically with the number of plants you have. In my first year or two of growing orchids, I can't remember seeing a single bug on the plants. That may be mostly because I didn't know what they looked like, but the few plants I had didn't seem to attract them.

Maybe they thought that so few plants weren't worth the effort and they were giving the new kid a break. But, when a friend pointed out some hard scale on some of my plants, I couldn't restrain a "So *that's* what scale looks like." I thought what I had were warts or something. Like new parents with their first baby, I didn't want to look too close for defects; what would I do if I ever found one?

SPEAKING OF SCALE, Malathion is OK, but Cygon 2E with its systemic action is much better. Knowing when the problem arises in your area will enable you to take specific aim at them and avoid spraying with everything, every month.

For those aphids that can spread virus, Mavrik is the primary control, but Orthene 75S, Cygon 2E, Dy-Syston and Dursban all do a good job. I am especially fond of Orthene 75S because it is available, broad-spectrum, very effective...and relatively cheap.

Use Safers Soap if the use of toxins bothers you or if you grow in the house. It won't affect your health (or the aphids', either, unless you use it for a long time; then, I think they just get tired of the taste and leave).

The insecticides listed above will handle the common insect problems you're likely to encounter with Phalaenopsis culture. It isn't necessary to use all of them at first, but look to a long-term program of keeping the little buggers off-balance with a variety of weapons. Plug in your local favorite bug-getters.

SLUGS AND SNAILS: The simplest and easiest way to keep away the slugs and snails is regular applications of a good molluscicide containing metaldehyde. I like Cookes because it is granular as opposed to the pellet-form. The pelletized stuff, by Ortho for example, is made of bran soaked in the active ingredient. The bran pellets usually take on a heavy coat of mold a few days after being wet the first time, something you don't need in an orchid pot. Only 3 or 4 granules of Cookes per pot are necessary if you are fastidious; a light scattering on the plants and surrounding bench area if you're not.

Remember to scatter some granules or pellets under the benches, too, for those who haven't made it up to the bench. Wire shelves are superior to wood laths or slats, incidentally, because they give the snails no place to hide underneath. A former local grower, Dr. Mark Dimmit, with tongue-in-cheek advocated dropping enough leaves and vegetative trash on the greenhouse floor to feed the slugs and snails in the hopes that they'd be satisfied with that and not bother climbing on the benches to get to his orchids.

An excellent and permanent (although somewhat expensive) barrier to the entry of snails and slugs is copper mesh or copper sheeting. Snails won't cross it. If you use it, be sure to set it in such a way as to prevent them from burrowing under. I've heard of copper cuffs around bench legs for this purpose. Copper screening on bench surfaces would be useful, too, if these nasties are a serious problem. (I think I just showed a sign of my age; when was the last time *you* saw copper screening.) Wrap several strands of bare copperwire around the legs if you can't find any screening.

Spray under the benches and in wet areas with a copper napthenate. (It's a good wood preservative although it makes the wood look moldy.) Copper and molluscs don't get along.

By keeping down the camouflage around the outside of your greenhouse, you can deter their entry. Cut back weeds, shrubs, and the like that give them a hidden entry to your growing area. (Again, if aphids are a problem as they are along the Gulf Coast of the US, use this same technique of ridding the area around your greenhouse of weeds.) A bait barrier around the exterior baseboard, such as Deadline, will check the bolder slugs and snails before they get in.

Slugs and snails are most pesty during cool, damp weather, so this is the time to begin the regular applications of the pesticide. Adjust that schedule as befits your local needs.

I keep an emptied, coarse-ground pepper shaker filled with Cookes granular snail bait in each greenhouse and scatter a little on any area that shows the telltale slime tracks of the disgusting things. (I had dinner in the posh dungeon of a German castle a few years back and was offered escargot as an appetizer. I inquired of the source of the delicacies and was told Fontana, California; 7 miles from my home. Someone was shipping the slimy little buggers out of country! I'd never thought of much beyond poisoning them or stepping on them.

Would you believe that a California university actually has a locally-common banana slug as its college mascot? Only in California! (And they don't call it a *banana* slug because it smells like one.) My lips are sealed; I'll never tell that it is the University of California at Santa Cruz.

Scatter the granules in an area several feet around each track to be sure. A visit to your growing area in the late evening, after dark, will give you some indication of the success of your snail snuff-out program. But, if you see something that looks like a brown banana, don't step on it; it might be someone's mascot.

Try to keep in mind that their gestation period is very short, 7-9 days for the brown snail, so go back after them a second time, 7-9 days after discovery of a track. If you're really mad, hit them a third lick, as well. Even if you're not mad, do it.

If you're building a greenhouse in slug/snail country, or considering it, include in your plans some snail barriers. Close all openings, particularly low vent openings at ground level. Screen all openings and pack any gaps where utility lines enter. Get 'em outside, don't let 'em in, and get the few that do get in.

(A side benefit of using Kocide 101 as I recommended in Section 6 is its copper nature. Slugs and snails avoid it because their mucus (slime) causes a electrolytic reaction with the copper and gives them a tingle. Scatter it on the floor where they are most likely to be. Go ahead, it's cheap. If you *still* need another reason to use the stuff, it does a good job of controlling algae on walkways in greenhouses...or elsewhere. And it lasts for several weeks.

Control really is not a time-consuming chore. Scatter the bait and that's it. That's enough on such a disgusting subject. I know, I know, people eat those things, but I don't even want to think about it, let alone do it.

I'll say this much for them: They know an awardable Phalaenopsis when they see one... that's the one they'll bite into first. At least it seems that way.

MEALYBUGS ARE MUCH, MUCH EASIER TO PREVENT THAN THEY ARE TO GET RID OF.

Regular use of insecticides which are 'specific for' (labeled as being known to control) mealybugs should hold the problem down to a manageable level. My wife, Nancy, keeps a 24-ounce spritz bottle of rubbing alcohol handy and sprays at any signs of the cottony, white webbing or the bugs themselves. Diazanon and Dursban work well on mealybugs. Also, anything with Metasystox will do well.

Read the label; it's worth your time, and the law requires you be told of the hazards of using some of these poisons.

Remember to adjust the pH of the water used in the pesticide solution to a little below neutral.

One *more* thing: Get into the habit of looking at the undersides of the leaves. That's where mealybugs and scale like to hang out...along with the mites which I'll talk about separately. Scale also will make themselves at home on the blooms of your plants, too.

MITES: Mites are critters so small you'll need a 10- or 14-power glass and a strong light to see, but you won't have any trouble seeing the damage they can do although the *pattern* is hardly recognizable to the unaided eye. The trace is a silvery stippling of the surface, the silver sheen provided by the tiny spider mites' webs.

They're a problem mostly in the warm, dry weather. Pentac does a good job for me, as does Kelthane, Morestan, Avid, Dycarb, Dursban, Mavrik and Vendex.

Mites can kill a plant in short order if not controlled. If a plant begins to lose more leaves than just an occasional one, be suspicious and look closely, particularly on the undersides of leaves. Be especially alert in warm, dry weather. Better still, mark your calendar and spray for the mites when you expect them to arrive...instead of waiting.

They're mostly red and mostly dead when you spray them with Kelthane, which is an old product and has a ridiculous on-the-market, off-the-market record in recent years in the US. I think the turmoil is over the amount of DDT in the material. New releases of Kelthane may have no DDT at all. The other products are much newer and probably don't have the horrendous effect on the environment that Kelthane does.

ONE ASPECT OF MITE CONTROL IS DIFFERENT FROM OTHER PEST CONTROL PROGRAMS. DON'T ALTERNATE MITICIDES.

Use one until it becomes clear that it isn't working, then switch to another. The reason is that simultaneous resistance to a number of miticides can occur, making control difficult. Do not raise the concentration of solutions above recommended levels as plant damage may occur. (Nelson,1981)

Although it boggles the mind, mites have been known to get inside closed Erlenmeyer flasks used for orchid seed culture. Researchers at UC Riverside found that the mites will follow mycelium of a fungus that grows through the cotton plug in the cap of the flask...and out the other side. The solution to this little problem is to mix a little Kocide 101 with vegetable oil and put a drop or two on the cotton plug. No fungus, no mites.

It just about blew my mind when I found spider mite damage on the leaves of seedlings in a flask I had received from a commercial nursery. I've found since then that the occurrence is not unusual.

KEEP PLUMERIAS OUT OF YOUR GREENHOUSE. THEY ARE MITE MAGNETS.

If the mite damage is active, you will also see live, tiny reddish-brown creatures...more kin to a crab than a spider...scurrying about. The tiny transparent spheres are eggs. While Vendex is still rated as the best miticide around, Morestan is right up there because it is also an ovicide (egg killer) as well.

Get a 10-power magnifying glass. Anything more powerful is too hard to handle and anything less is too weak. Edmund Scientific in Barrington, New Jersey has them for about $30. It's called a Cookes Triplet for the 3-element lens. Any field microscope of about the same power will do as well.

An intriging application of an old idea has found new support in recent years; the use of predatory or killer insects in growing areas. The new additions are predatory for specific pests including for scale and mealybugs.

Once introduced into a greenhouse, the predators will feast on the targeted pests until their food supply is gone. Unfortunately, then, they starve. If the pests come back, the predators must be replenished. (Sounds a little like American foreign policy, doesn't it!)

See your local agriculture agent for a source if you are interested in this natural form of pest control.

In addition to wiping out the pests that you have, the next best move is to prevent more from coming in, so

TREAT EVERY NEW PLANT AS THOUGH IT WAS INFESTED. It might be.

Spray the newcomers for every common pest and cut off the source of new ones. <u>You</u> may have perfect control of pests, but every other grower is a pig!

Gauge for trimming roots for a 5-inch pot.

Section 9. SETTING FLOWER SPIKES

Flowering in Phalaenopsis orchids is a response to an irritation or a stress caused (usually) by seasonal changes of light, temperature, and other external influences. It is a genetically-controlled sequence set in motion by too much or too little of the conditions the plant is comfortable with. It is a worried plant that flowers.

Flowering in Phalaenopsis orchids is caused by environmental influences. It must be stimulated; it doesn't happen on its own, but if we simulate the conditions that cause a Phalaenopsis to flower in the wild,

ALMOST ANY PHALAENOPSIS THAT IS CAPABLE OF SUPPORTING A FLOWER SPIKE WILL INITIATE ONE...

and all about the same time instead of dragging the process out beyond the time at which it normally would, as is often the case. Differences in the micro-environments of a greenhouse can cause a scattering of times of spike setting, even among plants of the same cross and age. That can be a problem for commercial growers as well as hobbyists. Adolescent plants that *can* bloom, probably *will*, given the stimulation I have in mind.

Although we may not notice the changes in growing conditions the plants undergo over a period of time, those changes *do* take place...even in the best-kept growing environment. These are changes brought about by the advancing season. Light levels and periods rise and fall, temperature levels rise and fall, and combinations of the two bring about flowering...with or without our knowledge or permission.

We usually notice the changes when something unusual happens, like when the greenhouse roof falls in or the heater quits. Almost everyone has had the experience or knows someone who has had a heater go out during a cold spell and, instead of finding the plants set back by the chill as might be expected, has seen them bloom better than ever in the following cycle. Scared hell out of them is what it did.

In Phalaenopsis, chilling temps below 58°F do not seem to improve flowering. When the plants are chilled to about 58 for 3 weeks, followed by the recommended higher light levels, you'll get all the flowering the plant is capable of producing.

Measured stress; enough to stimulate or irritate the plant, but short of doing any damage... just like exercise. Most orchids in culture more than 10 years or so start downhill and eventually just die. Ever wonder why so few of the old classics are still around?

While viruses probably account for some of the losses, I believe the main cause is stress or, more pointedly, the lack of it...arising from an overly-comfortable life style . Couch potatoes.

A lightly-stressed plant is more likely to maintain its ability to survive...from practice or exercise. A plant which is coddled and has every need fulfilled by its grower is one on its way down hill, like human couch potatoes...sort of. They've *forgotten* how to survive.

Among the highest achievers in human and animal society are those who stress themselves in an attempt to succeed...stopping at a point just short of a lethal dose. We know them as Type A's. Current research indicates that most Type A's who control their stress live *longer* lives, not shorter than the rest of us as was originally thought. There's a lesson there for us.

Lightly-stressed plants are healthy ones. No couch-potato orchids here. Bottom line: Some stress is good, like the stress of exercise for humans. Go easy, but don't eliminate it completely.

Exposure to a cold soak is necessary for many plants to flower, including grasses, some fruits and ornamentals. Snow Birds, cold-country retirees who flee to the warm climates, often bring their favorite tulips or other spring-flowering bulbs with them and find they must chill them in the refrigerator for a month to renew flowering. Otherwise, no flowers.

Flowers are a plant's sex organs. Did you know that? I didn't.

Unlike animals who are born with the vestiges of sex organs, flowers don't develop them until they're needed...to keep the species going. Plants do not enjoy the human animal's option for recreational sex. The flowers develop in response to an *outside* stimulus.

Without that stimulus, either low temperature or short day/long day, they will vegetate and never flower. These stimuli are heralds of season's change and are chapters in the life of the plant. They also present the plants with an opportunity to reproduce and preserve the species. Change of season is the cause of flowering.

The chilling process is called 'vernalization' or promotion of flowering by low temperatures.

Plants are capable of only two things, either vegetating (growing), or reproducing (flowering). They aren't smart enough to do both at one time, so it's one or the other. Chilling cuts short the growing cycle and induces the flowering cycle. So, in effect, you take over nature's role in telling the plant when to flower. You are flipping the life style of the plant over from growing to flowering.

Stimulation to flower in spring blooming phals is caused by low temperatures, short nights (and long days), or the two in combination. The cold soak triggers the flowering response; then, the quantity and size of the flowers is influenced by light intensity and duration...up to the point where light becomes harmful, other conditions being held constant. The trigger action is qualitative and the light following is quantitative in the process. Does that make any sense?

If the process is triggered by cold and subsequent light levels are not high enough to continue, the flowering process stops.

Flowering in a Phalaenopsis is an act in preparation for the death of the plant. It is almost a matter of life or death. For annual plants it *is* a matter of life or death, because they don't get a second chance. Perennials like orchids get more than one chance.

Mild winters in the temperate zones are usually followed by mediocre fruit and grain crops. Without a hard freeze, the act of vernalizing will not take place and wheat will not thrive the next season.

In the natural situation on western slopes in the Philippines, late autumn and winter bring a flow of cool, dry air off the Asian land mass. The flow sweeps out much of the warm, humid air and clears the skies in many areas. Daytime light and temperature levels rise with the removal of the clouds and haze; nighttime temperatures drop as the earth radiates more heat to deep space in the clear evening air; humidity falls in the relatively dry, crisp autumn days; rainfall is reduced; and air movement is increased as the dry masses of seasonally cool air flood the region.

Weather patterns, similar to the 'Indian Summer' of the United States with its bright, clear, warm autumn days...are common in temperate zones around the globe.

THEY MARK THE ONSET OF THE NATURAL FLOWER INDUCTION PROCESS FOR SPRING-BLOOMING PHALS.

While humans hardly notice small changes in light and temperature, plants pay close attention because they become uncomfortable...and are stressed or irritated. People just turn the thermostat up; plants get cold. If you don't believe me, go out and sleep on the lawn in your skivvies some night in late autumn. Like the plants, you'll start to wonder where your next generation is coming from.

Cultural steps taken to make or improve the flower induction process are best timed to boost the natural effect of the autumn seasonal changes.

THE TIMING OF THE ADJUSTMENT OF THE CULTURAL CONTROLS FOR FLOWER INDUCTION OF SPRING BLOOMING PHALS SHOULD BE KEYED TO THE CHANGE OF SEASON FROM SUMMER TO AUTUMN, WORLDWIDE.

The first day of 'Indian Summer' is a good marker, but, in tropical climates, the induction process should be started when clear weather, nighttime-outdoor temps fall to a range of 58-60°F or 15°C; *if* it falls to that level.

Most spring-blooming phals don't do well at sea level in the tropics. Surprised? I was. It doesn't get cold enough. Most phal species in the natural situation occur at or above 900 feet and below 1800 feet elevation.

SPRING BLOOMERS APPEAR TO BE STIMULATED TO BLOOM BY EITHER LOW TEMPERATURES OR SHORT DAYS...I'M NOT SURE WHICH. Probably both. They may also be day-length neutral.

SUMMER BLOOMERS APPEAR TO BE STIMULATED TO BLOOM BY LONG DAYS AND/OR SHORT NIGHTS...again, I'm not sure which and I don't figure on losing a lot of sleep worrying over which it is.

A question that has bothered me for a long time: Do Phalaenopsis plants at the equator have two flowering seasons because they experience two 'winters' and two 'summers' every 12 months? The sun angle is lowest when it is farthest from overhead to the north and again to the south...'winter'. It also passes overhead twice each year...'summer'. (I also worry about whether water in toilets at the equator goes clockwise or counter-clockwise. *Somebody* has to worry about these things!)

Because phal growers worldwide tend to keep their plants in the same temperature range, those plants induced to flower by chilling may bloom worldwide at the same time.

On the other hand, those induced to bloom by either long-day or short-day probably bloom in the season when the light levels reach the required length/intensity. The exceptions are those northern areas that have a lot of bright, sunny days and the southern areas that have lots of cloudy weather. (Aussies and Afrikaners flip the seasons.) Those grown under artificial lighting excepted. I'm not sure I understand what I just said, but I think the gist is that spring-bloomers flower at the same time worldwide. Summer bloomers flower earlier in the low latitudes.

(Is there a horticulture graduate student out there somewhere looking for a small demo project?)

Inducing the flowering of phals in culture involves some manipulation of (1) light, (2) temperature, (3) water/ humidity, (4) fertilizer, (5) air circulation, and (6) potting schedules. Let's look at how they can be adjusted.

ADJUSTMENT OF LIGHT:

RAISE THE AMOUNT OF LIGHT THE PLANTS ARE RECEIVING BY 25-40%
...from a norm of 1,000 footcandles(fc) to the flower induction level of 1,300-1,500fc, (measured with a meter, if possible), at solar noon. This is the time at which the sun's at its highest point in the day.

Maintain the increased light level for 6 weeks and return to the normal growth level of about 1,000-1,100fc. **IT IS IMPORTANT THAT THE PLANTS BE EXPOSED TO 3 WEEKS OR SO OF THE BRIGHTER LIGHT *AFTER* THE CHILLING PERIOD FOR BEST FLOWERING.** The closer you get to the 1,300 to 1,500 footcandles, the better the flowering you can

expect. That is the 'qualitative' aspect of light effect on flowering I mentioned earlier. Over 1,400 or 1,500 fc, you run the risk of damage.

(If you're going to use light in the range of 2,000 footcandles, and you can probably improve flowering if you do, use a higher rate of air movement and increase the nitrogen fertilizer during spike development to compensate for higher leaf temps and rapid growth.)

This is the way it happens in the natural situation such as in the Philippines...when the mass of cool, dry air advances south and then retreats back north with the season change. At this time, the clouds, humidity and rains return. This should tell you something about what the phals have been conditioned in the wild to expect. Matching those expectations is what culture is all about.

ADJUSTMENT OF TEMPERATURE:

INCREASE MAXIMUM AND DECREASE MINIMUM TEMPERATURES BY 5°F (3°C).

In most Phalaenopsis growing environments, this means setting new limits of 58 to 90°F from a norm of 63 to 85°F. While setting a lower minimum may be enough to cause spiking, many experienced phal growers agree that widening the daily temperature spread between the daytime high and the nighttime low...also helps. It may even work to compensate for those climates where nighttime minimums down to 58°F may not be a common occurrence.

Maintain the new temperature limits for 3-4 weeks, then return to the normal limits.

ADJUSTMENT OF WATER AND HUMIDITY: REDUCE WATER AND HUMIDITY.

Lengthen the watering interval a 'modest' amount. It is the time of year to do so anyway and flower induction is a handy way to remember the change. Lower the humidity to 50% or so, if possible. This will happen with reduced watering anyway, but a change in the misting system adjustment, if you have one, is in order, too.

If you can't lower the humidity, increase the air movement; it will produce a similar result.

The drier air in the greenhouse will make the wider temperature swing suggested above easier to obtain. Maintain the lower moisture level for 4-6 weeks.

ADJUSTMENT OF FEEDING PROGRAM: REDUCE NITROGEN FERTILIZER AND INCREASE THE PHOSPHORUS GIVEN TO MATURE PLANTS.

(All these adjustments need not be made to seedling culture; in fact, this induction exercise may set them back some, but not much.)

In the natural setting, reduced rainfall means fewer feedings for the plants of rotten bark, and bird- and monkey-doo, their usual rations. The simplest move is to stop feeding during this period, but if you continue feeding, use a high phosphorus fertilizer such as 2-10-10. If you are treating your tap water with phosphoric acid, keep in mind that you have already added some extra phosphorus...and that too much can be harmful.

Flush pots at the beginning of the period to eliminate as much nitrogen fertilizer as possible. Maintain this modified fertilizer program for 4 weeks.

Whether or not you give your plants fertilizer during the initial 4-week period,

FEED WITH EPSOM SALTS AT THE RATE OF 4 POUNDS PER 100 GALLONS OF WATER.

Five teaspoons per gallon for small quantities. (This step is not needed in locations where the water supply used has higher than normal levels of magnesium (24PPM), if dolomitic limestone is used to adjust pH or if foliar analysis exceeds .8% magnesium.)

Most growers can disregard this step, but if you are serious about getting all that is possible from your phal plants, use a high phosphorus fertilizer from the end of the first 4 weeks of the induction process until the time when the flower spikes are almost half developed (6-7 weeks). Then switch back to balanced for the rest of the year. (Some growers use a high-nitrogen fertilizer until the flowers begin to open.)

COMPENSATING ADJUSTMENTS:

INCREASE AIR CIRCULATION TO OFFSET THE HIGHER LEAF TEMPERATURES RESULTING FROM THE INCREASE IN LIGHT AND TEMPERATURE.

You turn on a fan or the cooler when you get warm, right? You certainly can do no less for your phals.

As is the case whenever making adjustments to the growing environment, look for the secondary changes needed to keep the plants comfortable and healthy.

FOR PHALAENOPSIS IN CULTURE, A BALANCE IN GROWING CONDITIONS IS NECESSARY. WHEN YOU CHANGE ONE CONTROL, LOOK FOR THE COMPENSATING CHANGE WHICH ALSO MUST BE MADE BECAUSE OF WHAT YOU OR NATURE JUST DID

like increasing light and temperature levels in the spring.

As you might suspect, the danger of bacterial rot is considerably higher during the time of the induction process, so begin the regular 4-week treatments with Kocide. Make the first application of Truban, Terramycin, or Dithane about this time, too. If there is any question of wet leaves at sundown during this 3-4 week chilling period, spray all your phals with Physan (or any similar broad-spectrum antiseptic), one teaspoon per gallon of water.

Do not increase nitrogen although it may seem called for; flower induction is an exception to the usual rule of high light-high nitrogen, low light-low nitrogen.

ADJUSTMENT OF THE POTTING SCHEDULE: REPOT IN THE WINDOW OF 60 TO 120 DAYS BEFORE THE BEGINNING OF THE INDUCTION PROCESS...if this is at all possible.

Add the impetus of the burst of growth that follows 2-4 months *after* repotting...to the flurry of activity taking place during induction. Repotting *within* 60 days of induction can reduce the rush that the plants experience during the process and dampen the total effect of the induction process.

By repotting 2 to 4 months before flower induction, all of the plant's excitement is concentrated in the month of the other steps and a doubling effect is achieved.

Do you think you need to be a little like a symphony conductor to make everything come out on time? (Or like the family cook?) Well, you *are*, you know. We try to imitate The Maestro in all this...and maybe this insight will give you a better appreciation of the beautiful symphony that is the Phalaenopsis orchid in all the glory of its full bloom.

HAVING SAID ALL THAT, CHANCES ARE GOOD IF YOU DO NOTHING OUTSIDE ORDINARY GOOD GROWING PRACTICES, MOST OF YOUR MATURE, HEALTHY PLANTSWILL STILL GO AHEAD AND FLOWER, ANYWAY.

But the steps I've outlined here will help ensure that *all* the plants that are *able* to flower...will do so and do it well. It is not uncommon to have plants with 3- and 4-inch leaf spans in bloom using this technique. It makes sense to cut these flower spikes off when you've seen what they look like, of course.

If these changes in growing conditions are what stimulate the Phalaenopsis to bloom...and there is sound reason to conclude that they do...it follows that the flower induction could be delayed by delaying the cooling period and the light increase and the other stimulants. It also follows that the flower induction process could be advanced by advancing these environmental changes. I can't attest to this because I've never tried manipulating the flowering process to suit my needs. But, I suspect it can be done. Similar adjustments are made elsewhere in the nursery business. It has also been done for economic reasons in the orchid business.

For those interested, see the text of an earlier book, *Phalaenopsis Culture: A Worldwide Survey,* Laid-Back Publications 1988, for more information. Particularly, see Woody Carlson's comments on the specific temperatures, number of days and other adjustments needed for precise flowering control.

It also follows that flowering should occur earlier in the season in cooler climates. That doesn't always happen because, while the stimulation to flower comes earlier, the less favorable growing conditions prevalent in the northern temperate zones slows the process down bringing flowering into about the same time window as that of the warmer climates.

OK, in making these changes to induce flowering, keep in mind that each change in cultural conditions probably needs a balancing change to keep plant things in harmony.

Balance is the key word here. See the notes on the next page on balance and the old Chinese principle of Yin and Yang applied to phal culture.

This wall of flowers is made possible through the use of step-benches; very efficient use of limited greenhouse space.

THE YIN AND YANG OF

PHALAENOPSIS CULTURE

(Corrections needed to balance the culture equation when changes are made.)

Y A N G

	LIGHT	TEMP	WATER	FOOD-N	AIR
LIGHT	N/A	INCR	INCR	INCR	INCR
TEMP	INCR	N/A	INCR	INCR	INCR
WATER	INCR	INCR	N/A	INCR	INCR
FOOD-N	INCR	INCR	INCR	N/A	INCR
AIR	INCR	INCR	INCR	INCR	N/A

(The word **Y I N** appears vertically to the left of the table.)

N/A= Not applicable   INCR=Increase or raise

When a control listed in the left-hand column is increased or raised, the control shown in the top horizontal column should also be raised...to keep the balance. An increase in Yin, must be combined with an increase in Yang to keep harmony. (How about a little Chinese cosmology on your phals. It's worked for them for nearly 10,000 years.) For example, if light is increased, increase also the temperature max, the watering, the humidity, the nitrogen fertilizer and air circulation.

THE REVERSE IS ALSO TRUE: WHEN A CONDITION IN THE LEFT-HAND COLUMN IS *LOWERED*, MAKE THE CHANGES OPPOSITE THOSE CALLED FOR ON THE CHART. On extended periods of gloomy winter days when the light level is down, lower the temperature a little, cut down on the nitrogen, let up a little on the watering schedule, and slow the fans down a bit.

I read somewhere that anytime you try to pick out something by itself, you find it hitched to everything else in the universe. That certainly appears to be true in Phalaenopsis culture.

The bottom line: when you raise one, raise the other; and vice versa.

WHILE WE'RE ON THE SUBJECT...

To conserve the plant's energy and force it to rest in preparation for a good presentation of flowers in the following blooming season, cut the flower spike off at its lowest point with a sterilized tool. Do this on the first day of the flower induction process...the beginning of autumn.

This step cuts the plant off from an enzyme produced in the nodes and tip of the spike...which keep the plant in the reproductive mode. Denial of the enzyme allows the plant to devote most of its energies to growth instead of reproduction, following a brief rest from its flowering labors.

DO THIS ONLY ON THE SPRING BLOOMERS! DO NOT CUT THE SPIKES OF THE SUMMER BLOOMERS. (See below) SUMMER BLOOMERS FLOWER MORE PROFUSELY WHEN OLD SPIKES ARE LEFT ON.

'Summer bloomers', those phals whose primary flowering season is in June, July and August in the northern hemisphere, are unaffected (and unharmed) by the flower induction processes detailed here. It is not necessary to separate them from their spring-blooming benchmates during the induction steps. There is reason to believe that they are stimulated to bloom by light rather than temperature changes and respond to long-day conditions of summer.

The following species, and their primary hybrids, bloom most frequently during summer months in the temperate zones:

amboinensis	fasciata
lindenii	venosa
corningiana	fuscata
mariae	violacea
cornu-cervi	sumatrana
lueddemanniana	

(This list may not help growers who have hybrids made with these species, because of the unpredictability of dominance of the flowering habit when they are bred with plants whose flowering season may be different. Bottom line: Don't worry about it. It's going to be all right.)

FLOWER INDUCTION SCHEDULE IN NORTHERN TEMPERATE ZONES#

WEEK	LIGHT	TEMP°F	FERTILIZER	NOTES
0 -OCT 8	NORMAL	62-85	BALANCED	
1 -OCT 15	HI*	57-92	FLUSH	HI*=1,300-1,500fc
2 -OCT 22	HI	57-92	EPSOM SALTS ONLY	
3 -OCT 29	HI	57-92	EPSOM SALTS ONLY	
4 -NOV 5	HI	60-92	FLUSH	
5 -NOV 12	HI	60-85	HI PHOS	
6 -NOV 19	HI	60-85	HI PHOS	
7 -NOV 26	HI	61-85	HI PHOS	
8 -DEC 3	NORMAL*	61-85	HI PHOS	NORMAL*=1,000-1,200fc
9 -DEC 10	NORMAL	62-85	HI PHOS	
10-DEC 17	NORMAL	62-85	HI PHOS	
11-DEC 24	NORMAL	63-85	HI PHOS	
12-DEC 31	NORMAL	63-85	HI PHOS	
13-JAN 7	NORMAL	64-85	BALANCED	

Southern hemisphere, add 6 months.

I don't know what the role of the Epsom salts is in all this. I've read the magnesium atom is at the center of the chlorophyll molecule and used in its synthesis, but beyond that, I haven't a clue. It certainly seems to wake the plants from a rest period and really get things moving...which is what we're looking for.

A possible clue: Epsom salts is primarily magnesium sulfate and magnesium serves as an activator for many plant enzymes required in the growth process.

Section 10. SEEDLING CARE.

PHALAENOPSIS SEEDLINGS REQUIRE CARE SOMEWHAT DIFFERENT FROM THAT OF MATURE PLANTS, BUT IT IS STRAIGHT FORWARD AND SIMPLE.

Many new growers shy away from raising seedlings because they fear the stories they've heard about problems with mature phals are magnified in the case of seedlings. As is often the case, only partly true.

In my experience, the reason why orchid people have problems with seedlings is that they try to treat them as mature plants...and as mature Cattleya plants, at that.

Most people learn what they know about orchid culture around their first orchids, which are usually catts. When the time comes to try a new genus, many will attempt to apply those same strategies that worked for them and kept their first plants alive and maybe even allowed them to flower well.

That's called riding a good horse. No matter that it was a different genus and an adult plant. Does that sound a little familiar? Is it any wonder that so many growers are leery of orchid seedlings?

I know a number of experienced growers who won't touch a seedling. "They always die on me" is the comment most often heard. It's not uncommon for such growers to experiment with several different genera and wind up with a collection of whatever survives the Standard Growing Technique...and no seedlings. ("That's the way I grow; if they don't like it, to hell with them.")

PHALAENOPSIS SEEDLING CULTURE IS CHARACTERIZED BY MODERATION.

Temperature minimums are higher and the maximums are lower; they like their little bottoms kept warm; light requirements are lower because they need more rest than adults and bright light forces them to grow; humidity needed is higher; the potting medium is finer; and they are watered and fed more often than adults. A lot like children, you say? You are correct. Surprised? Air circulation requirements are about the same.

Seedlings probably won't turn up their toes if you deviate a little from these norms, but the closer you stay to them, the more success you'll enjoy. Seedlings like a section of the growing area to themselves and control of the variables is a lot easier if you give it to them. Discussion following applies to community pots as well as separately-potted seedlings.

Section 10.1 SEEDLING CARE: LIGHT NEEDS.

Phal seedlings, when first out of the flask, need about 700 to 900 footcandles of light (7 to 9% of full summer sunlight), something over half that needed by mature plants and a little more when they've become adjusted. After they're established and up to 2-inch leaf span, give them the same light as the big ones.

Section 10.2 SEEDLING CARE: TEMPERATURE NEEDS.

They need 75 to 80°F or 24 to 27°C. They like it on the high side of that range when they first come out of the flask, if you get them that way. Down a bit after they're settled. Wherever possible, give seedlings *bottom* heat to keep their roots warm. Heating tubes under a wire bench or an electric heating pad made for this purpose work just fine.

Section 10.3 SEEDLING CARE: WATER NEEDS.

If they're in small pots, they'll require more frequent watering to prevent the medium from drying out. There is a direct relationship between the size of the pot and the interval at which they should be re-watered...small pot, small interval.

DON'T LET SEEDLINGS DRY OUT.

They have virtually no reserves to call on if deprived of their basic needs...and water is one of their basic needs. Daily spritzing for the first 3 weeks out of a flask is useful and not excessive. The venerable Roy Fukumura of Maui advises spritzing every day with water and every third day with a solution of SuperThrive (Vitamin B-1) followed immediately with a water spritz to move the good stuff down to the roots. I might add that it is quite dry where Fuku-san lives in Kahului.

The constant moisture they require is going to pose a special problem with fungus and bacteria. They need regular applications of a fungicide-bactericide, starting as soon as they leave the flask. Physan works okay, but its detergent action tends to leave seedling potting medium a little soggy, so pay particular attention to the drainage holes in the pots.

Don't use the Physan or its generic equivalent any more often than every 10 days or so; then at the rate of one-half teaspoon per gallon. I think it has a toxic effect if over-used, particulary on seedlings. Seedling pots need extra drainage, just like the pots used for the big guys. (See Section 5 for details.)

Physan is all right if you're keeping down the number of chemicals you use on your plants, but I believe that Natriphene does a better job. Natriphene is a pain in the butt to make up in small quantities, so I usually use the Physan, but some time back, I made up a gallon of Natriphene and I use it in place of Physan on occasion to keep it from getting old. The Natriphene is to prevent damping-off in seedlings.

The best gauge of how often to water seedlings is, again, the hand method: Pick up the pot and heft it. Watching them closely helps. One day without water and they may go limp. Seedlings love automatic watering or misting systems...that always remember to water them.

I recommend pre-soaking the potting medium used with seedlings in a dilute Physan solution like with the bark used with mature plants. I usually dump a 5-gallon bucket of hot water, to which five teaspoons of Physan concentrate has been added, into a 30-gallon plastic barrel full of seedling mix.

Section 10.4 SEEDLING CARE: POTTING MEDIUM.

The best all-round mix is fine fir bark, but there are others that are also good. It works well all by itself although some growers add other ingredients which include charcoal, lava rock, styrofoam, cork, redwood, sphagnum moss (including the New Zealand variety which seems to suit seedlings very well), Perlite, vermiculite and some other things that fall into the category of weird.

If you live in a dry climate, I suggest using the small grade of Perlite with the fir bark at a ratio of 5 parts fir bark to 1 part Perlite. Holds moisture better.

The bagged mixes of coarse sphagnum and Perlite are also good for dry conditions, but be careful of over-watering. (Walt Cousineau of WC Orchids in southern California got me started using Fison's Sunshine Mix #1 and I like it. It's a Canadian product made in Vancouver, BC.) I like to add fine fir bark to this mix. Don't ask me why; it just seems the right thing to do.

Some Hawaiian growers use a mix of Perlite and coarse sphagnum moss and grow their seedlings in clay pots. The clay pots work well in a high humidity climate, but are not satisfactory for climates outside a maritime belt, an area from the coastline to about five miles inland. They dry out too quickly and accumulate salts which can damage tender roots. Because they also evaporate moisture through the clay, they also get a little cooler than the plastic...bad news for seedling roots that like to be kept warm in the winter. Make it easy on yourself; use plastic pots, instead.

If you use square 4-inch plastic pots as community pots, you can snap on those plastic tops that come from markets on strawberry baskets. They make a nice, little micro-environment that holds in moisture and slows temperature changes. Check to see if they're holding too much moisture in, though, and limit their use to about 4 to 6 weeks. Algae and rot take over after that.

THE RIGHT AMOUNT OF MOISTURE IN A PHALAENOPSIS POT IS A BALANCE THAT IS AFFECTED BY THE FREQUENCY OF WATERING, THE DENSITY OF THE POTTING MEDIUM, THE TYPE OF POT, NUMBER AND SIZE OF DRAIN HOLES, AMBIENT HUMIDITY, TEMPERATURE, AIR CIRCULATION, WETTING AGENTS APPLIED, AND OTHER FACTORS.

If you are going to experiment, change only one variable at a time and hold the other things constant. Otherwise, you can draw no valid conclusions from whatever happens, good or bad.

Section 10.5 SEEDLING CARE: FERTILIZER NEEDS

A balanced fertilizer such as 20-20-20 or 18-18-18 will work just fine. Use the material at one-quarter the recommended strength and apply at every watering. A complication: As the medium gets older, the plant will get more nitrogen from the deteriorating organic matter and will need less from fertilizers added.

You will get faster growth with high nitrogen fertilizer such as a 3-1-2 ratio, but growth will be softer, a condition which could make disease more possible. This problem can be offset by increasing the light level by 10-20% or so to make use of the added nitrogen. If you use a high nitrogen fertilizer, alternate with a balanced fertilizer to reduce the probability of soft growth. See Sections 3.5 and 4 for other information on fertilizers for Phalaenopsis.

IF SEEDLINGS DON'T SEEM TO GROW STEADILY AND THE OTHER CONDITIONS RECOMMENDED HERE HAVE BEEN MET, UP THE AMOUNT OF NITROGEN YOU'RE FEEDING THEM.

The pH of your water or potting media could be denying nitrogen to the little guys. Suggested: add one-quarter to one-half a cup of sulfate of ammonia to a 5-gallon bucket of fertilizer concentrate for use with a Syphonex...if your light is good. If it isn't, the sulfate of ammonia will make the seedlings grow too rapidly and they will get soft and prone to disease; wait until the light gets better, say up to 800 to 1,000fc. More light, more nitrogen. Less light, less nitrogen. Archie Bunker would assert that this point should be chiseled 'inedibly in your memory.'

NEVER APPLY ANY CHEMICALS, INCLUDING FERTILIZERS, TO A DRY PLANT.

If it's dry, water first and fertilize the next day. If you can't do that, don't feed them until the next watering. The potting medium will hold some nutrients, so the plant won't go short. If the fertilizer shock doesn't kill the plant, the ugly fertilizer burns on the leaves will be there for a long time to remind you of your indiscretion.

Section 10.6 SEEDLING CARE: POTTING THEM.

Don't be in any hurry to remove seedlings from a community pot even though they may look a little crowded. The little dickens' like each other's company and grow better crowded up to a point. A real problem with leaving them too long in a compot is that the big ones will over-shadow the smaller ones, denying them light and hiding any problems the little ones may have. Try to leave phal seedlings in a compot until they're at least an inch in leaf spread.

Another problem with leaving phals too long in compots is that if one gets sick, the others will shortly, too. Pseudomonas can wipe out a

compot overnight, so watch seedlings a bit closer than you would the older ones. Just like babies.

Avoid un-flasking phal seedlings during the short-day season. Hold off until spring if you can. Temperature extremes are fewer and the light is better and longer and they are just beginning a surge in growth. As an added bonus, you have a shot at their blooming the following spring-summer.

First flowering of a seedling is not uncommon at 16-18 months out of the flask. Expect most at 24 months or so. The laggards will go 3 to 4 years, but don't give up on them. Many a grower has been fooled by mediocre first bloomers that were followed by much better late bloomers. Most of the awarded Phal. Misty Greens, for one, were in that category.

Don't throw them away if they aren't gorgeous in their first blooming. Most Phalaenopsis plants don't produce their mature-best flowers until their third blooming.

Many people are intimidated by orchid seedlings in a flask and will not buy them and are deprived of one of the more rewarding aspects of orchid culture. It isn't so much the little tads in a bottle that is frightening; it's the thought they must come out before they can flower that is.

The scientific nature and appearance of an orchid flask intimidates many into thinking that this sort of thing is best left to the professionals. Maybe so for some, but the scene of an orchid grower with his/her first de-flasking operation under way is not unlike that of new parents with their first-born. Giddiness is the first term that comes to mind.

Grow your phals in glass just as you would in pots except for light, and hold that to about 500 footcandles or about 4 inches from double fluorescent lamp tubes. All the other criteria for seedlings listed herein apply. However, don't bring your flasks into the greenhouse. There are micro-organisms floating around freely in the greenhouse that *can* be drawn into a closed flask. Keep them where it's uniformly warm and where they'll get 10 to 12 hours of fluorescent light each day.

When the majority of the seedlings in a flask are an inch or more in leaf spread, it's time to deliver them into the Real World. Open the flask and fill about half-full of tepid water. Swish gently to dissolve and loosen the agar. Pour the whole mess out into a plastic sink strainer, the kind about 9 inches in diameter with little holes or slots, and run or spray tepid water over the little seedlings to wash off all traces of the flasking medium. Some growers soak the new seedlings in a sugar or very weak fertilizer solution to give them a boost.

Put about an inch of mature plant bark, pathway size or 1/2 to 3/4ths of an inch, in the bottom of a 4-inch square pot and cover that with another inch of seedling mix. Set the pot at an angle in loose seedling medium in a shallow box or bowl (15-18 inch is good) and put a small handful of mix or sphagnum in the lower corner.

Lay the seedlings on the top edge of the mix in a row across the pot about an inch apart. Add more seedling mix to cover the roots of the row of seedlings. Repeat the process for 4 or 5 rows with 4 or 5 seedlings in a row. Press down gently on the medium to compact. Right the pot and run tepid water gently over the seedlings and the mix to settle everything. Add more medium as necessary, because after watering, everything will have settled a bit.

An alternate method to this one is to fill the pot with first coarse, then fine mix, to the top. Then, using a pencil as a dibble stick, poke little holes an inch or two deep and insert one or more of the plant's roots. Only one root is really needed, so don't waste a lot of time trying to get them all in the hole.

Spray thoroughly with room-temperature Physan (1/2 tsp per gallon) or Natriphene and snap on a strawberry box top. Don't cover the pots with film plastic as an alternative to the strawberry covers. There must be some ventilation. Keep the cover on the pot between waterings for 5-6 weeks and remove it. That's long enough for the seedlings to adapt if you pot out during the spring. Leave it on too long and you invite fungal and bacterial problems.

Keep them warm as noted above.

The best time of year to decant seedlings is in the spring when days get longer and warmer. Repeat the Physan or Natriphene spray every 2 weeks for the first 2 months or so until the danger of damping-off is past. Treat them as any other seedling from that point on.

One convenient way of handling the neo-natals is to bring the little community pots of them into the bathroom and keep them on a bright windowsill for several weeks. Keep a spritz bottle handy with a weak fertilizer solution (one-eighth recommended package strength) and give them a shot every morning before you put your pants on. Add a little sulfate of ammonia (a quarter-teaspoon per gallon) for quicker growth. A little SuperThrive here couldn't hurt. It may not help, either, but a lot of smart people I know use it.

Loss of some seedlings from any given cross is not uncommon. Don't be unduly concerned unless the loss rate exceeds 10-15%. The smaller the seedlings are when removed, the higher the expected rate of losses. Additionally, there are some genetically weak seedlings in almost every group. Some crosses are difficult to grow and losses may go higher, much higher in some cases, like violaceas. It's probably just as well they go when they do. They'd be difficult to handle later anyway.

Phal seedlings, fortunately, aren't like your kids; you can trash-can the ones you don't have time or space for. With few exceptions, the puny seedlings never make it to flowering, no matter how much care they get.

Satisfy yourself that is true, then move on and don't waste your time trying to save the weak ones. It isn't hard to see that some seedlings are going to fall by the wayside for one reason or another. For this reason and the others above, you can see why many people, mothers especially, don't want anything to do with seedlings. Nancy chokes up every time she has to throw some of the tiny ones away.

You may be getting an insight to why the orchid produces upwards of a million seeds and, in some cases more, in an attempt to survive. Don't let this frighten you off. Try seedling culture. It's difficult only until you learn how. It's also a pre-requisite to hybridizing and raising new crosses.

BOTTOM LINE: (1) THE CULTURE OF SEEDLINGS IS DIFFERENT AND YOU MUST LEARN SOME NEW RULES AND (2) WEAK CLONES USUALLY WON'T SURVIVE NO MATTER WHAT YOU DO.

Strawberry box cover used to make
a mini-greenhouse for seedlings.

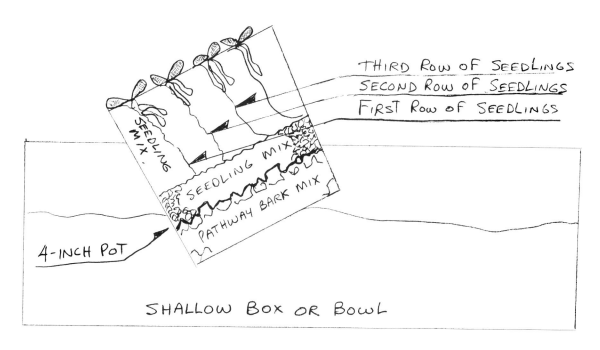

Set-up for potting seedlings.

Section 11. PROPAGATION.

When you acquire good phals, maybe even have some of your own awarded by the American Orchid Society or another judging authority, you probably will want extra 'copies' of them to sell, to give or trade with friends and, certainly, to have as a back-up should some disaster befall your original plant. Because they are monopodial (one-footed), phals cannot be divided as can cattleyas, paphs and a multitude of other orchids. But all is not lost,

THERE IS AN EASY METHOD BY WHICH ALMOST ANY HOBBYIST CAN CREATE DUPLICATES OR CLONES OF THE ORIGINAL PLANT.

It's a simple matter to make one or two clones, but if you want larger quantities, you have to resort to a lab technique which requires a sterile environment, for starters, and materials and tools not available to most hobbyists. There are commercial labs that handle this work at a relatively modest $10-12 for each 'stem propagation' or clone. (They're called 'stem propagations' or stem props because the clone is made or propagated from a node on the flower stem.) Many societies have one or more serious hobbyists who do lab or tissue culture work and may be qualified to help you.

Back to the simple technique to make one stem propagation at a time in your own growing area. All that is required is a razor blade, a toothpick and some 'keiki paste'. I use the keiki paste made by Dr James Brasch, Box 354, McMaster University, Hamilton, ONT L8S 1CO, Canada, and am quite satisfied with the results. Jim retails some other chemical

magic things, too. See the AOS *BULLETIN* for his regular ad.

Keiki paste is a cell-division stimulant suspended in lanolin. The active ingredient in most formulas is 6-benzylaminopurine or BAP which is readily available at the larger laboratory chemical supply houses.

BAP is also used in seed flasking to cause proliferation of scarce embryos and in the stem propagation technique alluded to above, among other purposes. The difference between a 'stem propagation' and a 'mericlone' has never been formally defined by any orchid authority, but is generally accepted to be a matter of numbers of clones produced; large numbers of clones made at one effort are considered mericlones where small numbers, usually one or two, are considered to be stem props.

The difference in numbers is usually determined by the amount of BAP used in the flask. More BAP, more little ones = mericlones. Often no BAP is used and just one stem prop is produced.

The late Jack Grimes wrote an interesting article on how to make stem props in a plastic soda bottle without sterile conditions. (See Vol 56, Number 4. April 1987, p. 369.)

I haven't tried the technique, but it looks easy and Jack says it is.

In any event, what it does when applied to undeveloped nodes or 'eyes' on Phalaenopsis flower stems is cause the node to begin to grow and develop either as another flower spike or as a keiki. Good timing and luck have a lot to do with which you get.

(Serious hobbyists take note of another technique recommended in the December, 1984 issue of the AMERICAN ORCHID SOCIETY *BULLETIN,* The In Vivo Propagation of Phalaenopsis Orchids by Dr. Rob Griesbach.)

THE TECHNIQUE: With a sterile razor or any sharp blade, cut lightly from one side to the other through the bract, which covers the undeveloped nodes on a phal flower spike. Sterilize the blade in a flame. The node is round, so cut in an arc around and under the node and lightly! Make a smile-shaped cut.

You only want to cut away the bract-cover without damaging the tissue underneath too badly. Practice on a flower spike you can afford to screw up, first. Be careful not to damage the node. There is a school of thought that says to deliberately mutilate the node a little...and it will pop a keiki out of sheer panic. Maybe so, but every one I've tried died. I don't do that anymore.

Protect the node and, with the bract off, (remove it with tweezers if some threads still hold it on) you're ready for the keiki paste. Smear a little on the uncovered node and the incision you made with a toothpick – and that's it.

Wait a couple of weeks to see what happens. If nothing, repeat the paste trick. If a flower spike erupts instead of a keiki, let it develop and apply keiki paste to the nodes on the new spike when buds differentiate. Figure on a 50% success rate as being a good average. I have the best results when I make the attempts late in the blooming season. Done during the shank of the season (March-June in the northern hemisphere), most will produce another flower spike, something a mature plant will try to do anyway.

I believe it is important to know what is on the plant's 'mind' when you try to start a keiki. A mature plant, not pollinated during first flowering, will usually flower again, sometimes to the detriment of the plant if it isn't strong enough to carry another flowering.

The plant's first priority is propagation of the species, to make babies. Pollinated flowers, given their way, produce lots of good seed and, thereby, lots of chances to proliferate; second best (this usually happens when growing conditions are something less than ideal), is to produce one offshoot, a natural keiki. The third strategy is to preserve its strength for a run at flowering next year.

Asexual propagation, or reproduction without a flowering phase, is not nature's first choice. Production of seed is far better from an evolutionary standpoint because each seedling is likely to be a little different from the others and this diversity of genetic material is nature's way of producing mutations, any one of which could improve the species' long-term chance of survival. There is an evolutionary advantage in sexual reproduction; there is none in vegetative propagation, the method we're talking about here...(no fun, either). If you attempt to cause a keiki during flowering time, a strong plant will produce another flower spike and bless you for kicking things off. If you try when it's getting ready to bed down for a rest till next season, your chances are better of getting a keiki, because the time for flowering has gone by. Think like a Phalaenopsis would, okay? ...are you still with me? Yoo hoo!

Lightly stressing the plant appears to increase the likelihood of a 'take' in this method of plant propagation, just as it does in the case of flower spike initiation. To this end, move the plant up into somewhat brighter light and higher temperatures and watch it closely after application of keiki paste. As soon as the keiki appears, relieve the stress by moving the plant down into cooler, more moist growing conditions.

Dr. Steve Pridgen recommends squirting a little solution of gibberellic acid (1:5,000 in distilled water) in leaf axils and on undeveloped nodes to encourage keikiing. I have no idea why, but I've had several startling successes with the trick. Maybe just coincidence, but a big phal, with a 'stalled' plantlet, started growing again 2 weeks after a slosh of gibberellic acid...and this after being dormant for at least 2 years. Ditto on keikis starting with only the gibberellic acid stimulation.

Gibberellins will cause flowering in some species of long-day plants which flower in a manner similar to Phalaenopsis...but there is nothing in the literature to suggest that phals are among those that do. (Salisbury, 1971) If you want to tinker, make up a little of the 1:5,000 solution, pour it into a 'pik' used by floral arrangers, cap it and slip the tube over the end of a free-flying root on a summer blooming phal. Leave it there until the root absorbs all the solution. I've had it work several times...I think. If nothing else, it's fun watching the water level in the pik go down as the root drinks.

Remove a keiki when it has a total of at least 4 inches of root showing. (One 4-inch root or four 1-inch roots or any combination thereof.) Break it off or cut carefully with a sterile blade, spray with Physan and pot it normally.

Breaking the keiki off probably makes more sense, because it eliminates one contact with a cutting tool and one opportunity to transfer virus. Gail Wisler pointed out in her book on virus control that the reason for the very low incidence of virus in paphiopedilums could be the practice of breaking divisions away from the main plant instead of cutting them. Makes sense.

Relieve the stress on the newly-potted keiki in the same way as above. We're talking about some heavy duty stress on the little dudes, so anything you can do to make life easier for them is going to improve your success rate.

Post-partum care is the same as any comparable-sized seedling. Keep the keiki paste in the refrigerator between uses. It will maintain its pizazz longer.

Sometimes a happy phal will produce an offset or plantlet, a clonal growth from the trunk of the plant below the bottom or next to the bottom leaf. It comes from an undeveloped flower spike node and is genetically identical to the parent or to a keiki originating from a flower spike. Handle as above. Spray the injured tissue on both the parent and offspring with Physan solution after separation and before potting as a precaution.

Something you may want to think about is letting a friend hold your 'insurance' plant or backup to a good original. He or she can be using and enjoying it and, if you should lose your original (unlikely but possible) you have a fall-back position and need only call the friend to get back into business...hopefully.

Another advantage of this practice is that you'll be able to see, in a very practical way, how good your culture is relative to another's and where you may need to make some changes. If your friend does any breeding with the plant, the usual arrangement is that the original owner gets a flask or compot of the progeny.

We'll talk about another use for the keiki paste method of propagation in Section 12 where we aren't trying to make another plant, but trying to save the one we have. This is an emergency measure and a last ditch attempt to save an otherwise kaput plant. Let's get on with it.

A keiki growing from a phalaenopsis flower spike.

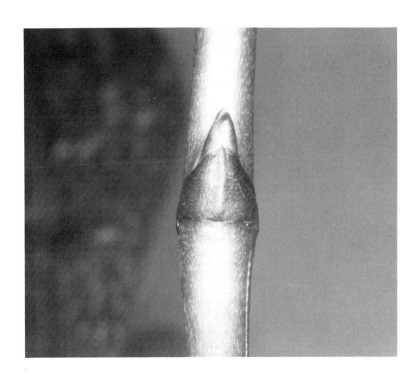

Phal flower spike node...untouched.

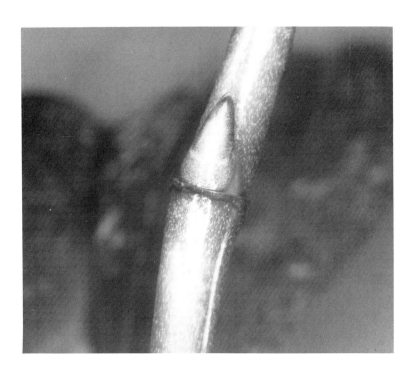

Phal flower spike node...bract removed.
Ready for keiki paste.

Section 12. SOME COMMON PROBLEMS AND HOW TO SOLVE THEM.

No FLOWERS:

If you have a healthy, mature plant that will not bloom, chances are good it is not getting enough light.

Where you place the plant can be very important, particularly if you are growing them in the home. A south window or exposure is best, but be careful not to burn them; east is the next best; and west is the third choice. Northern exposure does not give enough light for phals to bloom decently; sometimes, but not usually. (Unlike African violets, whose culture is similar, Phalaenopsis will sometimes bloom in a northern exposure, but seldom will they do it well.)

A second possible cause for failure of a mature, spring-blooming phal plant to bloom is that the plant has not been 'cold-soaked' by 4 to 6 degrees below their normal minimum of 61 to 63° F. in the autumn. The 'cold soak' must last 3 to 4 weeks, followed by 2-3 weeks of brighter than normal light.

Phalaenopsis schilleriana is notorious in the Philippines for not blooming in the city of Manila during its normal blooming season of February through March. It keikis instead. Manila is essentially at sea level whereas the schilleriana is found in nature at or a bit below 750 feet above sea level...where nights in the fall get quite a bit cooler than downtown Manila...about 10 degrees. The sad story happens over and over when people buy the lovely schillerianas in bloom or bud in the hills and bring them to the city...never to see them

flower again. (Valmayor, 1984)

If you have a schilleriana that won't bloom: During the flower induction period starting on the first day of autumn, try giving it more light, more moving air, a little less nitrogen fertilizer (or none), keep it a bit dryer, and make sure it sees a 25 degree F. difference between day and night temperatures. They also like to be grown a little cooler than other phals. Can you see why these beauties are not happy at sea level? Surprised? Me too.

That may not always do it, but you should see some blooms, other things held normal. The bottom line is to try to match what nature gave it originally. (If you have a phal mariae that won't bloom or won't bloom well, decrease the light. They don't like a lot of light.)

If you have a lueddemanniana that blooms in some years and not in others, rest easy. There's a lot of us who don't understand why, either. One clue may be that plants kept high, 'near the glass', may not see the low night temps in the fall unless top vents in the greenhouse are opened.

Try bringing them down to bench or ground level during the chilling process in October and November. I don't have any great conviction that will help. I've done it and had the plants bloom, but I'm not really sure that the reason was what I did. It seems as though they bloom two years in a row and then skip one. When they bloom, they *all* bloom at once. Bottom line: don't get too concerned if your lueddemannianas don't bloom every year.

For more on the subject of getting these stubborn summer-bloomers to flower, see Section 3.

Too much nitrogen fertilizer may also prevent the plant from blooming. They really don't need very much nitrogen. If you're technically inclined, they need 100 parts per million (PPM) in constant feeding that is, feeding with every watering.(Poole and Sheehan, 1980) That equates to a tad under 5 ounces of 18-18-18 fertilizer in 5 gallons of concentrate for use with a Hozon proportioner...not very much. This figure applies only if you fertilize with every watering.

One other possibility for failure to flower, among others: The plant may be too immature. Immaturity is different things to different species. A 10-year old gigantea could well be immature. But most phals will bloom by the time they're 3 years out of the flask, if they are otherwise healthy. The 'rabbits' will bloom in sometimes 14 months out of the flask.

CROWN ROT: (Pseudomonas cattleyae)

Crown rot is a bacterial disease caused by standing or persistent water in the cup-like crown of the plant. To cope, water early in the day, tilt the plant, spray with Physan to speed drying and protect from a proliferation of harmful bacteria on the leaves and crown. Raise the temperature, if possible, if the plants are damp at sundown.

If you lose the crown of a plant to crown rot, all is not lost. Very often, if you do nothing other than spritz a little Physan, R-D-20 or Naccosan B-60 or even dilute Lysol in the crown, a new plant will grow from the sick one...but not always. Sometimes the process needs a little help.

One ploy when the crown has gone on a phal to crown rot and there are still some green leaves on the plant (This is often the case, especially if you stop the infection with a bactericide before the rot has destroyed the trunk.):

Unpot the plant and wash it clean; spray the whole thing with Physan solution, one teaspoon per gallon of water. With a sterile blade, cut the base of the top leaf remaining, but stop short of cutting more than just past the center of the base of the leaf. Cut it to a point where the leaf comes in contact with the trunk.

THE OBJECT IS TO BARE AN UNDE-VELOPED FLOWER SPIKE NODE WHICH IS UNDER MOST LEAVES, BUT NOT TO LOSE THE LEAF.

You'll need it to produce food for the plant during its recovery. Sometimes you can see a bulge in the lower extremity of the leaf where it flares around the trunk. The bulge may well be a node, but not necessarily. Cut well down on the flare of the leaf base to avoid damaging the node underneath. Make a second cut to remove a triangle of leaf tissue and expose the node. See photos.

If the nodes have all been used to make flower spikes or if no nodes appear, smear the keiki paste on the tops of the roots where they join the trunk. I don't know the reason, but I've had the latter technique (of putting the keiki paste on the tops of the roots) work several times since Bill Livingston suggested it. Apparently there are some undifferentiated cells around the root exit from the trunk that are stimulated by the keiki paste to make new growth. These cells are just waiting to be told what to become, be it a leaf, a root or a flower spike. It's like magic.

When a node is exposed, smear a little keiki paste on it...and invoke the deity. Keep the plant a bit drier than usual and increase the light by moving it up toward the glass. This is the same technique recommended for routine keiki formation and, you're right in thinking it probably is stressful for the plant. But, that is the idea. Frighten the plant into acknowledging it is in serious danger and hoping it will respond with a survival move...by making a keiki. You tread a fine line in stressing the plant this way, though. You can kill it altogether. Stress it just a little, okay?

If you haven't gotten a keiki to form by the time the leaves fall off, you've had the schnitzel and so has the plant. Note: They sometimes will go for a year or more in this state of limbo before they (1) produce a keiki or (2) die. Repeat the keiki paste after a month if nothing has happened. Hit all the root tops this time, just in case. It can't hurt.

Once the keiki initiates, move it back to normal bench-level *seedling* culture. Do only one node on the first pass. I've had several take on the first try and watched the plant die from an overload of new growth.

If the plant is sound other than the loss of the growing point, this technique is successful more often than not. Saving half of those good plants that would otherwise go belly-up is a fair return on the investment of time and effort.

Once the node initiates new growth, the whole plant will begin to pick up because a hormone is produced in the growing point which energizes the entire organism. Treat it like the young plant it is from then on. Don't make the mistake of putting it back with the other mature plants. You may wipe out the new growth.

THIS IS A VERY USEFUL SURGICAL TECHNIQUE, BUT PRACTICE ON A CADAVER OR TWO BEFORE IT BECOMES NECESSARY TO USE IT.

Other times, I've done this same treatment *without the surgery* and had the plant throw a keiki.

PSEUDOMONAS INFECTION:

Pseudomonas cattleyae is a BACTERIAL infection that is common, but is easily controlled if you have a little understanding of what is going on. It appears as a dark green spot that appears wet. It is caused by standing water or a break in the skin of the plant. The pathogens or germs are usually present on the skin of the plant...and this is the reason for a preventive program we discussed in Section 6.

The safest fix is to cut off the diseased part of the leaf (if you can) and spray the raw edge with Physan. Try to get 3/4ths of an inch of green, undiseased tissue on the severed part. That's still no guarantee of stopping the advance of the disease, but usually it will. If it persists, repeat the action taking more good tissue this time.

If possible, save the leaf for the plant by cross-hatching the diseased patch, bottom and top of the leaf with a sharp, sterile blade and spray with Physan. Get a deep score between the diseased spot and the crown to prevent further advance. See photos. If the infection is within two inches or so of the crown, don't fool around with it. Cut it off and take no chances. I've done this cross-hatching technique hundreds of times and *it has not failed once.* When the tissue dries out, you'll have a hole in the leaf, but at least, it is functional and the infection is stopped. My thanks to Ed Wise for this one.

106

Bill Luke, D.O., of Phoenix, has a novel technique, albeit an effective one, of coping with the sad sight of a rotten socket left when crown rot strikes a Phalaenopsis plant. Its real value lies in being able to get to the bacterial pathogens inside the trunk or the stump of a phal whose top leaves have rotted and dropped off. He injects .3 to .4 cc of Gentamicin directly into the infected area with an insulin hypodermic syringe. The cost of Gentamicin is now down to about $3 for a 2 cc vial. Unfortunately, Gentamicin is a prescription drug, but the insulin syringes can be gotten without a prescription. If you have access and the plant is worth the effort, let it not be said that crown rot is a terminal problem. Perhaps a family practice doctor in your society could help. Follow up by stimulating an undeveloped node to make a keiki.

My standby, that usually works, is to squirt a few drops of 1:1 solution of Difolitan into the dead tissue of the crown to stop the rot. Physan, Kocide and Subdue will also work, but with varying degrees of success.

MULTIPLE LEAF DROP:

Any time a Phalaenopsis plant has more than one dead leaf on it, be alerted that something is probably wrong. Unpot it and examine the roots and the medium for problems, but especially in dry weather, look at the undersides of the leaves for signs of spider mites. Those little stinkers can kill a plant in short order if not restrained with a little Kelthane, Morestan or Pentac.

If you haven't had the problem, become familiar with the appearance of the silvery, pitted surface any way you can, like checking your friends' phals for mites in the warm weather. (You can really endear yourself to your friends by looking for bugs in their collections with a magnifying glass.) As long as you have phals, you're going to have mites to one degree or another, depending on your alertness to the problem and your quick application of miticide.

I've noted in my travels around the Phalaenopsis world that there is a strong correlation between the ownership of a good magnifying glass and the number of mite infestations.

Only the people who own the glasses have mites. You can interpret that one any way you want to.

THE MAJOR DIFFICULTY IN CONTROLLING MITES IS THAT YOU CANNOT SEE THEM AND MUST RELY ON YOUR ABILITY TO RECOGNIZE THE DAMAGE THEY DO.

If you run across a type of mite that isn't controlled by either Morestan or Pentac, try Diazinon. Some mites are not controllable by the usual means...like bud mites.

Some leaf loss is, of course, normal. It is simply the process of the old leaves dropping away after having served out their useful lives. But, **MULTIPLE LOSS OF LEAVES IS NOT NORMAL AND CAN BE AN INDICATOR OF CULTURE PROBLEMS** such as the mite problem referred to above.

LEAF LOSS CAN ALSO BE CAUSED BY A LACK OF NITROGEN.

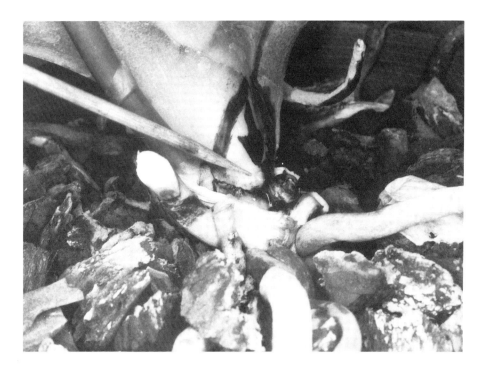

Uncovered, unused node. (barely visible at
tip of pointer) Triangle of tissue has been removed.

Same as above. Node is visible
at the tip of the scalpel.

If you live in an area where the pH of your tap water is high, **NITROGEN NOT ONLY MAY BE DENIED TO YOUR PLANTS, BUT PROBABLY WILL BE EVEN IF YOU ARE FEEDING THEM REGULARLY.** You may need to acidify your water before use on the plants. A quick call to the water company should provide an answer to this question. I referred to this situation in the section on water and water quality.

If you have strongly alkaline water and you are not yet acid-treating, it sometimes helps to supplement your regular balanced plant food with a small amount of sulfate of ammonia, the ordinary stuff used to green up lawns in the spring.

Between March and November in the northern hemisphere, try adding a quarter to half a cup of it to 5 gallons of fertilizer concentrate used with a Syphonex. Don't be surprised if you see a burst of growth along with an end to the leaf loss problem. But do the acid treatment first. The sulfate of ammonia actually lowers the pH of the fertilizer water a bit.

I can't prove it, but I think the sulfate of ammonia also has an effect on multiple spiking. It certainly seems so. But, be careful of overusing it. Too much can cause toxicity. Stick to a quarter- to half-cup per 100 gallons.

Alkaline water, with a pH above neutral, can cause a deficiency in phosphorus. This is also a common cause of multiple leaf loss. The answer is to acid treat your water or use the sulfate of ammonia above. Although there is no phosphorus in it, during breakdown sulfate of ammonia forms an acid which lowers the pH of the fertilizer solution...and makes more of the phosphorus available...and may stop the multiple loss of a plant's older leaves.

SOFT LEAVES: Soft leaves are usually caused by dehydration, and dehydration is caused by either (1) not enough water or (2) too much. Not enough water is understandable, but too much water will cause root rot ...which denies water to the plant...and causes dehydration.

Too coarse a potting medium will also cause the problem. Repot in *fine* mix as a therapeutic measure, and treat as a seedling. Adding Perlite to the mix helps, too.

ANY TIME YOU HAVE A SICK OR WEAK PHALAENOPSIS PLANT, PUT IT INTO SEEDLING POTTING MEDIUM OR NEW ZEALAND MOSS AND TREAT IT AS A SEEDLING.

Fine potting mix is the chicken soup remedy of the Phalaenopsis world. Another reason to learn the specific needs of seedlings is that the same regimen of care is used sometimes on mature plants, albeit hurting ones. Don't worry about getting too much moisture or causing root rot by using the fine mix on mature plants. Good drainage provided by the extra holes and frequent repotting as detailed in Section 5 will prevent most problems of this sort.

DROOPING FLOWER SPIKES:

There isn't much you can do about this one; it is in the nature of some Phalaenopsis adult plants to flower on long spikes. (The better to get the attention of prospective pollinators) Any phal that has big pinks or whites in its background will usually have this problem...if in fact it is a problem in the usual sense.

If you are going to have a problem, that's the kind to have. (I once knew a lady who had one leg half an inch shorter than the other and, by legal definition, was a handicapped person; but, you should have seen what that missing half-inch did to her rear-end action. Handicapped, hell! Like I say, if you're going to have a problem...)

About all you can do with drooping spikes is to stake or tie them up during their development and turn the habit into one of hallmarks of elegance for which phals are noted.

THE RULE OF THUMB IS TO STAKE AT OR JUST BELOW THE LOWEST FLOWERING NODE OF THE SPIKE.

This is often the fifth node up from the bottom. Do this while the spike is forming and chances are it will take on the magnificent arch that is so characteristic of large pink or white phals or progeny of them.

IF YOU INTEND TO SHOW THE PLANT, DO NOT MOVE IT FROM ITS ORIGINAL POSITION AFTER THE FLOWER SPIKE HAS BEGUN TO GROW.

Most phals will try to face the sun when they flower. If the plant is moved after the spike has taken its original set, the flower buds will twist toward the light and the magnificent arch will look more like a dog's hind leg. If you must move a plant after the spike has gotten past about one-third grown, try to set it back into the original orientation with respect to the sun. Some people paint an index marker on the pots to show which side should face the sun.

The small, plastic inertia reels called NIE-CO-ROLs are nigh on to being perfect for handling those long phal spikes. Ann Gripp at Santa Barbara Orchid Estate in Santa Barbara,

California has them, occasionally. (They're made by a very small concern in Holland. Apparently it doesn't take much to cause the firm to shut down production for a while, so the supply is a little erratic.) The NIE-CO-ROLs continuously adjust themselves as the spike grows. Otherwise, the usual staking method will do. Wire stakes with a U-shaped bend at the top are handy.

If you are self-sufficient, wire stakes are easy to make from number 12 or 14 galvanized steel wire. I buy the wire in 100 pound rolls (and use it for a million things). I cut it into lengths of from 8 to 20 inches after straightening it out from the coils it comes in, then put the U-bend on with a pair of lineman's pliers. They probably cost me about the same as they would have if I bought them, but I get a psychic income from self-sufficiency, and, also, I can make them to exactly the size I need.

Jack Woltmon in Hawaii gave me the answer to straightening the wire for use. Cut a 20-30 foot length of looped wire. Set one end in a vise and the other in the chuck of a variable speed 3/8ths inch electric drill. Hold firmly and turn on the drill, slowly at first, until the wire twists and straightens, probably about 100 turns for a 25-foot length.

The wire will be as straight as a die if you pull back on the electric drill while it's turning...and stiffer, too, because it will work-harden in the process. Cut into lengths with small bolt cutters or lineman's pliers. Neat.

Shorter phal spikes need to be staked, too. Some, like the short-spiked violaceas and some of their primary hybrids will rest their flowers on their leaves. That's neat sometimes, but more often than not they will look better facing the viewer. If they're hung

NIE-CO-ROLS in use.
(Phal. Sarah Frances Pridgen "Shamrock" AM/AOS)

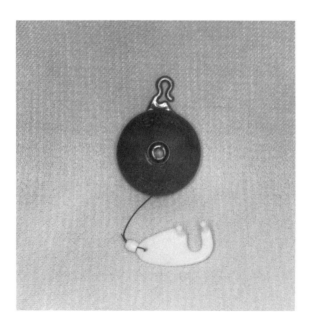

NIE-CO-ROL (Inertia Reel).

high, no problem. If they are at bench level, though, make a short stake with a U-bend on it and point their little faces toward their admiring public.

Incidentally, my violaceas grow very nicely hanging at about 5 or 6 feet above the greenhouse floor and have an uncluttered view of the light. They grow well there and I can tilt the crowns to keep water from collecting because they're hanging from a wire rod.

I find that most of the summer-blooming species grow better if elevated to 5 or 6 feet off the floor in the greenhouse.

SMALLER-THAN-NORMAL FLOWERS IN FEWER-THAN-NORMAL NUMBERS:

Most of us have had the experience of buying a plant in glorious bloom and never again seeing the likes of that original flowering. (If you are a cymbidium grower, you know exactly what I mean) Some of that is due to cultural and chemical magic done by the nurserymen who grew the plant in the first place, but often it's because we don't know how to keep them happy.

One of the steps necessary to regular, abundant flowering of phals is an enforced rest period or at least a rest from the labors of blooming excessively. A mature, healthy phal will try to bloom more than once in a growing season. (I've read that phals don't really rest at any time; they just don't work as hard. Somebody's quibbling.)

That's a nice habit that phals have, but it can be hard on a plant, too, because it will keep on trying sometimes when it should be resting and getting ready for the next season. Many will terminate flowering naturally by drying up the spike...and it's not those I'm discussing now.

The way to force a phal to rest, when it doesn't want to, is to cut off its flower spike, below the bottom node. If you don't, you may wind up with the problem of smaller-than-normal flowers in fewer-than-normal numbers that is the subject of this paragraph. Cut back the OLD, not the new, spikes on spring bloomers about the beginning of autumn and the summer bloomers about the beginning of winter.

Other reasons for smaller flowers than normal can include too much light, not enough fertilizer, too cool growing conditions, disease, repotting during spiking and any other form of trauma during the growing season.

Most phals take 2-3 years from their first bloom to reach full maturity at which time the flower size and numbers should stabilize and repeat yearly thereafter if they remain in good health. It's amazing sometimes how a plant will improve after its first flowering. A puny, little pink Phalaenopsis with one flower that my wife paid eight bucks for got an Award of Merit (AM) from the American Orchid Society 2 years later. That drives nurserymen crazy.

SHORT SPIKES; SMALL, HARD BLOOMS:

Too much light. Chances are good the leaves are leathery and yellowish in color, too. Cut back the light, especially after spikes have initiated.

BROWN, DEAD TISSUE ON THE LEAVES:

Could be sunburn. If it happens on a recurve surface of the leaf that is at, or close to, 90 degrees or perpendicular to the sun's rays, chances are good that is the problem. A recurve surface on a leaf is that area where the leaf curves down both in length and in breadth, leaving a relatively flat spot. The tops of your ears and your nose are recurve surfaces, too, and they also sunburn easily.

Sunburn destroys useful leaf tissue, but usually will not harm tissue outside the original burn. I've had Pseudomonas develop on the margins of a severe sunburn. If you have a leaf flat up against a window, you may well find it sunburned because no cooling air can circulate across its surface.

Not to worry. All the damage that is going to happen has happened, and that's it. Cut off the damaged tissue if it offends you, but there is seldom valid reason to remove functional leaf tissue. When it is diseased or when you want to show the plant, perhaps; but otherwise, leave it on. It's working for you and for the plant. Oh, move the plant from the bright light, too.

DRY, BROWN SPOTS ON LEAVES:

Dry brown or black spots on the leaves of phals sometimes are Leafspot, a fungal disease caused by Cercospora sp. Spray Dithane M-45 on the plants during the cool weather. A handy way to remember to do it is to combine the Dithane with the Kocide 101 I recommend for control of Pseudomonas cattleyae. The two materials are compatible.

FLOWER SPIKE COLLAPSE:

This one drove me bonkers until John Miller told me what it was and what was causing it. Scenario: A phal flower spike grown to three-fourths full size, with differentiated buds showing, suddenly goes soft and collapses, turning black within a few days. The time is January through March in the northern hemisphere. The problem is thermal shock (or mesophyll tissue collapse) and it's caused by

the splashing of cold water on the warm, tender, new flower spike.

When splashed on new leaves the cold water causes deep pitting, but no spread of the malady. It is a thermal reaction and carries with it no persistent disease. Warm plant tissue is shocked by the cold water and it dies in reaction; sort of like frostbite in humans. The damage usually affects new, soft plant tissue only.

If your tap water temperature goes much below 60° F., you need to take some corrective action. You have several alternatives if you've got the problem of cold water that is to be used on your phals: (1) heat some water to be added to the stream of cold water coming from the tap through a Hozon syphon; (2) allow water to approach room temperature in a tank or container of sorts before use or; (3) water with the cool water, but be careful not to splash it on new tissue in leaves or flower spikes. (Difficult if you have many plants)

Sometimes, if your water line to the greenhouse is close to the surface of the ground, it will run colder for the first 15-30 seconds that the tap is open, then warm up a few degrees as the water from the deeper-buried main line comes through. So, try running the water a little and see if the temperature rises.

Speaking of water pipes. This is probably not the best place to interject this point, but it will do: When you build a greenhouse, use at least a three-quarter inch feed pipe for water. Half-inch is just too small and causes all manner of flow problems. Three-quarter inch pipe has 2.25 times the cross section of half-inch and probably carries twice as much water. Back to cold water. John Ewing Orchids uses a solar heater to warm the water. Stewarts, as I mentioned earlier, uses a bucket of hot water and a modified

Hozon in the phal stud house. If you are a solar-energy buff, think in terms of black plastic pipe and a closed solar heat collector box, and let your imagination run.

Pesticides, especially Diazinon, sprayed directly on new flower spikes and buds can cause bud drop and sometimes it will kill the spike. Keep pesticides off the tender tissue.

If you have mealybugs on flowers, spray with some rubbing alcohol. Zap! Works right now, but has no lasting effect...except on the bug you just sprayed. Repeat as necessary...on the flower, not the bug.

One move that helps out here is to spray with the strong stuff just before flowering season and hope the effect lasts until the flower spikes harden. It usually will if you use a systemic pesticide such as Cygon 2E or Orthene 75S.

SEPAL WILT:

There will be times when the top sepal of a Phalaenopsis bloom will lose its moisture, become semi-transparent and collapse before it would normally. The other two sepals are usually affected after the top one and the petals not at all. The usual cause is contaminated air and the main malefactor is ethylene gas. A natural gas leak or an exhaust gas leak from a defective heater should be the first suspect, but heavy smog can cause it too. (Smog can also cause seed capsules to abort, too.) If you suspect a gas leak, call the gas company. Gas company service people working in a neighborhood can release enough gas to give a house full of flowers a whole lot of trouble.

Sepal wilt only affects opened flowers...usually. Buds are not affected at all unless the leak is very bad. Plants aren't threatened until the gas concentration gets very high.

Rotting fruit, especially apples, can also create enough ethylene gas to cause problems. The gas also accelerates the decaying of other apples and probably gave rise to the homily "one rotten apple in a barrel..."

BUD DROP:

New, emerging flower buds are very vulnerable to damage from changes in their environment. It's easy to kill them off by getting careless. A swing in temperature up to 100 or down to 55°F can wipe out a sizeable part of your bud population.

Bud drop is caused, among other things, by warm drafts, cold drafts, too much light, gas (butane, propane or natural) leakage from a heater, gas company repairmen working in the local area, roofing contractors working in the area (asphalt vapors), cold water, hot water, pesticides, lower temps than normal, higher temps than normal, insufficient nitrogen, too much nitrogen, dryness, soft growth from low light and warm temps...see anything there you like? In short, many things can harm the little darlings when they first emerge, so be on your toes during this critical time and

AVOID ANY CONDITION OUT OF THE ORDINARY.

Buds are the newest and tenderest tissue in the plant at this point and the weather is at its lousiest. They don't like a lot of change at this stage, so baby them a little, OK?

All this talk of problems with phals is pretty dreary and, be realistic, there are some very real problems with growing them. But, on the other hand, we've discussed most of the things that could give you trouble and they *are* controllable, given a bit of thought. It's a small price to pay for the immense personal pleasure that comes from growing *real* orchids.

114

Cross-hatching technique for
stopping Pseudomonas infection

Cross-hatched leaf...
Pseudomonas arrested.

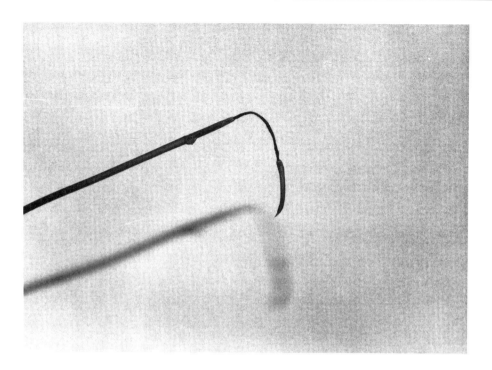

Flower spike killed by thermal shock.

The problem here on the desert:
High temps and low humidity.

Solenoid valve (isolation), Merit Commander fertilizer injector,
fertilizer concentrate bucket, and output to zone solenoid valves…
for an automatic fertilizer injector system.

Fertilizer zone solenoid (shutoff) valves.
Note caps on ends of the tee for expansion of the system.

Section 13. PROGRAMMED CARE

Note 1: The following recommendations apply when the season is normal or average. If the season is cooler, cloudier, brighter, or warmer than the norm, make necessary adjustments to this schedule.

Note 2: Regarding insect control, it is well to make note of times in the season when pests appear in your growing area and annotate this schedule to treat for prevention of those pests in that time only. There is little point in spraying for the little buggers when they aren't there to appreciate it.

Note 3. A bright, clear, cloudless day in June at this latitude (32 degrees north) will read about 10,000 footcandles of light. One thousand footcandles equates to about 10% of that light with 90% shade, if that helps to visualize the situation. Otherwise, use the formula suggested in Section 3.

Note 4. This schedule applies to the northern hemisphere. Add or subtract 6 months for the other hemisphere.

Note 5. For keeping track of this information as well as just about all the rest that is necessary for disciplined growing, consider using a culture record book. The one made by orchidPhile of Stamford, CT is a good one. The pages come in grades of complexity starting with the information beginners need to keep track of and go up to a much more detailed account for the serious record keeper. I've had this problem with memory since I passed 40, so I am a big fan of good records. Takes the guesswork out of growing. Good move.

JANUARY

Light	1,000 to 1,200 fc
Temp	62 to 64° min. (but they like 68°F much better)
Fertilizer	High phosphorous
Pot?	Only summer bloomers
Insect control	Local requirements
Disease control	Spray with Kocide once or Physan twice

118

FEBRUARY

Light	1,000 to 1,200 fc (and increase shading to compensate for lengthening days.)
Temp	65° min.
Fertilizer.	Balanced
Pot?	Only summer bloomers
Insect control	Local requirements
Disease control	Kocide or Physan

MARCH

Light	1,000 to 1,200 fc
Temp	65° min.
Fertilizer	Balanced
Pot?	No
Insect control	Local requirements
Disease control	Kocide or Physan

APRIL

Light	1,000 to 1,200 fc (increase shading to compensate for lengthening day.)
Temp	65 to 85°
Fertilizer	Balanced
Pot?	No
Insect control	Local requirements
Disease control	Kocide or Physan

MAY

Light	1,000 to 1,200 fc
Temp	65 to 85°
Fertilizer	Balanced
Pot?	Maybe
Insect control	Local requirements
Disease control	Probably none, but watch

JUNE

Light	1,000 to 1,200 (increase shading to compensate)
Temp	65 to 85°
Fertilizer	Balanced
Pot?	Yes
Insect control	Local requirements...mite season
Disease control	Check local requirements.

JULY

Light	1,000 to 1,200 fc
Temp	65 to 85°
Fertilizer	Balanced
Pot?	Yes
Insect control	Local requirements—check for mites
Disease control	Check local requirements

AUGUST

Light	1,000 to 1,200 fc
Temp	65 to 85°
Fertilizer	Balanced
Pot?	Yes
Insect control	Watch for mites
Disease control	Local requirements

SEPTEMBER

Light	1,000 to 1,200 fc
Temp	65 to 85°
Fertilizer	Balanced
Pot?	No
Insect control	Local requirements
Disease control	Kocide or Physan
Added	Cut back flower spikes except summer bloomers

OCTOBER

Light	1,300 to 1,500 fc (Remove shading)
Temp	55 to 85°
Fertilizer	Balanced
Pot?	No
Insect control	Good time for a systemic pesticide such as Cygon
Disease control	Kocide or Physan
Added	Note flower induction schedule in Sect. 9.

NOVEMBER

Light	1,300 to 1,500 fc
Temp	60 to 85°
Fertilizer	None
Pot?	No
Insect control	Second spraying of a systemic pesticide
Disease control	Kocide or Physan
Added	Note flower induction schedule in Sect. 9.

DECEMBER

Light	1,000 to 1,200 fc
Temp	62 to 64° min.
Fertilizer	High Phosphorous
Pot?	Only summer bloomers
Insect control	Local requirements
Disease control	Kocide or Physan
Added	Merry Christmas

Step-benches; underside view.

Staking a phal flower spike.

CHAPTER THREE

Beside good care

Section 14. THE NEED FOR BALANCE.

(YIN AND YANG AND THE CULTURAL EQUATION OF ORCHIDS.)

I'm going to make one point in this section...and one only. Note it now and you can relax for the rest of the 20 minutes or so it takes to read it:

WITH PHALAENOPSIS *IN CULTURE*, ANY CHANGE YOU OR THE SEASONS MAKE TO YOUR GROWING CONDITIONS...REQUIRES A COMPENSATING ADJUSTMENT TO KEEP YOUR CULTURE IN HARMONY.

When it gets cold in the house, you turn up the thermostat. If it's too dark, you turn on the lights, right? Same principle. And that's it. For the rest of the section, I'm going to elaborate on that bit of cultural advice.

My frame of reference is, as you might suspect, the Phalaenopsis..but most of what I have to say here applies to any orchid...or any plant in culture, for that matter.

Very simply put, Yin and Yang are two opposite sides of a balanced situation. The principle of balance embodied in Yin and Yang has been used by the Chinese for 10,000 years to guide their lives...and to ensure a bountiful rice crop.

Yin refers to things feminine, passive, cold, wet, dark. This principle combines with:

Yang which embodies things masculine, active, warm, dry, and light. These two, in balanced combinations and intensities, form all the good things that come to be.

For example, a balance between man and woman; between active and passive; between warm and cold; between wet and dry, between work and play and between light and dark. This balance was...and still is to many...the guide to a life of harmony and happiness. They believed that when a living thing was out of harmony with nature or their fellow beings, illness or trouble would result. (They were primitives and we're modern people, right? Sure, sure.)

Unlike the western principle of dualism, where light is good and dark is bad, Yin and Yang don't oppose each other, but rather they *complement* and grow out of each other.

And there is a lesson for us in orchid culture here: A balance of all influences can lead to healthy, prosperous plants. Plants need some light and some dark; they need some warmth and some coolth; some wetness and some dryness; and so forth.

Moderation in all things, I think is the way at least one philosopher put it.

There are five controllable variables in orchid culture; light, temperature, water/humidity/fertilizer, potting medium and air circulation...and they need to be kept in harmony with one another because they are interrelated. Change one and you will need to change others of the five some...because we have reason to believe everything is tied to everything else in the universe.

Nature makes these adjustments for plants in the wild. In culture, the job is yours. That's the point of this section.

Some of these culture balancing adjustments are obvious; others not so.

Harmonious growing conditions are like a cultural equation: If one side is changed...the other side must also be changed to maintain the balance or the equilibrium; assuming, of course, that you had a stable or harmonious condition to start with. If you didn't, refer to one of the cultural textbooks (preferably mine) and start this process with conditions in your growing area where the plants are reasonably happy.

When I talk about balance, I don't mean only to lower the temperature when it's too hot and reduce the light when it's too bright. Those things are obvious to most growers, but, I'm also talking about such things as raising the humidity and nitrogen feed when the light is very bright and lowering the humidity and nitrogen when the light's very low...and so on. There are more. We'll talk about some.

I don't think there is any more dramatic illustration of the need for balance in orchid culture than in the use of fertilizers.

Excessive use of some nutrients can reduce, or 'antagonize', the uptake of others. The most common so-called 'antagonisms' are shown in the graphic. So much for the argument that you can feed your orchids all the fertilizer you want because they will only take up what they need. That's like saying if you drink cyanide, no problem because your body will take in only what it wants. A foliar analysis should answer any questions you have on your use of fertilizers.

ANTAGONISMS

Antagonizor	Antagonizee
Nitrogen	Potassium
Potassium	Nitrogen
	Calcium
	Magnesium
Sodium	Potassium
	Calcium
	Magnesium
Calcium	Boron
	Magnesium
Magnesium	Calcium
Iron	Manganese
Manganese	Iron

Note in some cases the antagonism is reciprocal; if you use too much nitrogen, for example, you can induce a deficiency in potassium...and vice versa.

The rules I'm going to discuss apply mainly to culture under natural light. Growth under artificial light requires some modification of these ideas. We'll discuss those later.

You and your body make adjustments almost constantly in an attempt to keep the equilibrium of your health and comfort. You shiver to generate heat when you're cold; you perspire to cool off when you're too warm; you wear sunglasses and a hat when it's too bright outside. A plant's ability to make that kind of adjustment in a short period of time is very limited (But, many will, given enough time. The process is called evolution.), so it will be up to you to do it for them; that's what 'culture' is all about. In the forest, either the plant adapts or it dies. In culture, either you adapt or it dies.

It is important to know and match natural growing conditions of the main species in your plants...because you will need to match those conditions if you are to give the plants exactly the conditions they would like to have or are accustomed to having. Death of a plant is nature's way of telling you it was unhappy with the way you were doing things.

OK, let's talk about some of the specifics:

WHEN LIGHT IS INCREASING AS IN THE SPRING AND THE SUN ANGLE GETS STEEPER:

Hold the light level at about 1,000-1,200 footcandles by fine-tuning, preferably with shade compound. Shade cloth is a clumsy substitute. Check light levels every 3 weeks or so throughout the year and adjust the shading as necessary.

When you're using a light meter like the GE model T214, which many growers use, place the meter on the bench...or hold it parallel to the surface at leaf level. Tilting the meter will give a bum reading on the high side. I've met growers who insisted they were growing their phals at 3,500-4,000 footcandles, but when we looked at the way they were measuring the light, we found they were pointing the meter toward the sun...instead of pointing it straight up as the instruction sheet indicates.

Shade cloth does a lousy job of controlling light with any degree of finesse. If you leave it on all year, your light level will be right twice a day for part of the year, once in the spring and once in the fall. Just like a broken watch is right twice a day. It has only two levels of use, off and on. Taking the shade cloth off in the winter is an improvement, but shade compound is a much easier and cheaper

method, and gives you almost unlimited control of the light. Shade cloth, or any other fixed means of regulating light, can't do that.

BACK TO OUR EXAMPLE, WHEN LIGHT IS INCREASING IN THE SPRING,

raise the average temperature in your growing area. Raise it to match the increased number of light-hours available. Don't be in a hurry to turn the cooler on or open the vents, but don't let high daytime temps exceed 85°F, either. Let the afternoon temperature rise to 75-80°F., if it will. The increase in temp will allow faster, healthier growth.

AGAIN, AS LIGHT IS INCREASING IN THE SPRING,

raise the humidity and shorten the interval between watering. Obvious? Sure, but many of us don't do it, especially the part about raising the humidity. The increased moisture feeds fast growth, lowers heat stress and gives some protection to the plants from peaks of over-heating. It also cools them and permits you to give the plants more light without burning them. More light (up to a point) means faster and stronger growth and better flower production.

MATCH THE AMOUNT OF FERTILIZER GIVEN THE PLANTS TO THE AMOUNT OF LIGHT THEY ARE GETTING.

In this case increase the feed as the light-hours increase. The plants will be trying to grow rapidly at this time and need the nutrition. They *don't* need it when they aren't growing, so you can cut back on feed then.

Note: If you have very bright light, even in

the winter as is the case in latitudes closer to the equator and a few special cases such as the prairies of Western Canada...you will need some nitrogen even in the shortest days of winter to permit the plants to use the light for optimum growth.

Phals probably grow throughout the year with little or no rest, but they grow faster in bright light and warm temps. The extra nitrogen, especially, will permit the plants to grow at the max rate possible. I'm presuming that is something you want.

ONCE AGAIN, IN THE SPRING,

increase air circulation to cool leaf surfaces that will be heated up by the increase in light and temperature. It will also help dry off surface moisture quicker and lower the possibility of bacterial and fungal disease which could arise with the increase in water and humidity, mentioned earlier.

THE RULE IS THE MORE LIGHT THEY GET, THE MORE AIR CIRCULATION THEY WILL NEED.

That's how it happens in nature.

For example, about the first of December a large mass of cool, dry air off the Asian land mass moves all the clouds and moisture out of the area around the Philippines...giving the plants more light. Remember the discussion in the section on flower induction?

Frank Fordyce is fond of saying that we should listen to what our plants are telling us. If they aren't prospering, change what you think is bothering them. I know that sounds so simple as to be insulting, but many of us don't pay attention to what the plants are telling us and

grow them the way *we* want rather than letting them grow the way *they* want to.

About these adjustments, I'd like to suggest an old fighter pilot's rule: When something goes wrong, un-do the last thing you did... quickly. It couldn't hurt to keep track of any changes made in the greenhouse in a journal of sorts. I can't remember where I put my glasses 5 minutes ago let alone remember what I changed in the greenhouse a month ago. They say the knees go first, but don't you believe it!

This rule applies whether the light increase comes from a seasonal change or any other reason such as when a heavy rain washes off a lot of the shade compound or when you remove the shade cloth. For example, if you remove your shade cloth a little earlier than you should, like after a week of cool, cloudy weather in early October in the northern hemisphere, your plants will *fry* when the sun comes out. In this case, turn *up* the air circulation to keep leaf surface temperatures down...and check to see if other measures are necessary, like raising the humidity.

ALL RIGHT, LET'S LOOK AT THE REVERSE OF SPRING CONDITIONS... LIKE WHEN THE MAX LIGHT INTENSITY IS FADING IN THE AUTUMN.

Remove shade compound to try to hold the light level at 1,000-1,200 footcandles as long as you can. If you are going through the steps of flower induction, wash off most of the shade compound about the first day of Indian summer (or the first day of autumn) and increase the light to 1,300 to 1,500 footcandles and hold it there for 30-45 days. By then you'll probably have to take it all off anyway to maintain 1,000 or so foot candles.

THE 900-1,000 FOOTCANDLES IS A MINIMUM LIGHT LEVEL FOR GOOD PHAL HEALTH AND GROWTH, BUT LESS THAN IS NEEDED FOR OPTIMUM GROWTH.

When the plants are getting less light as a result of the advance of autumn, lower the daytime high temperature permitted. The idea is to slow the growth rate and avoid soft growth and the likelihood of disease...which will result from warm temps and low light. This adjustment also is useful during a protracted cloudy spell. Same kind of a problem; same kind of a solution.

An exception to the rule: If you are deliberately inducing phal spikes, expand the temperature window by raising the daytime max by 5 degrees F., (3°C) and lowering the nighttime minimum by 5 degrees(F.) for the same 30-45 days as in the previous step...*then* lower it.

Does all this talk of measuring light imply that I think a light meter is needed for good phal culture? You bet. The 70 bucks US or so you'll pay for the General Electric T214 meter will come back to you many times over. If you have been at this for 35 years and have calibrated eye-balls, you may not need one. Otherwise, you may find yourself stumbling along in the dark, so to speak.

OK, BACK TO AUTUMN ADJUSTMENTS:

Back off on watering and lower the humidity. If you've been using a misting system during the summer because of low humidity, lower the humidity level demanded. If you've had plenty of humidity during the summer, but suffer from dryness in the winter, turn the misting system *on* now.

As a general rule, we've got less light to dry the leaves off now and air at a lower temperature will hold less humidity, so to avoid root rot, bacterial and fungal problems, we'll need less moisture.

But greenhouse heaters have a way of drying things out too much. So, if your growing area has low (below 50% relative humidity) in the cool weather, continue the misting process. I suppose you've guessed you need a reasonably accurate humidity gauge, or hygrometer. If you've been waiting for someone to tell you to go buy one...I'm telling you now.

In nature, the same thing happens. When the rain quits, the humidity goes down.

The reduced rainfall also cuts down on the bird droppings and monkey-doo that get washed down onto the plants, the natural process of fertilizing. To match this phenomena, **REDUCE THE AMOUNT OF FERTILIZER GIVEN,** especially the nitrogen you feed the plants.

Growth has slowed at this point so they don't need much, and there's enough tied up in the potting medium to provide what little they need over the next month. The elimination of nitrogen for a 30-day period is one of the key steps in phal flower induction. It's like fasting before the Big Event.

CUT BACK ON AIR CIRCULATION TO SAVE POWER AND TO RAISE THE 'APPARENT' TEMPERATURE.

For flower induction, hold normal air movement for the 30-45 days, *then* reduce it. Do not drop below the level where disease could become a problem. That means keeping enough circulation to move cigarette smoke in the corners...just a little.

OK, that's what I mean by compensating adjustments for changing *light* conditions. Are you getting the feel for balance...and harmony? Can you see the forces of Yin and Yang at work here? Change one; keep the harmony by changing the other.

Let's deal with adjustments necessary **WHEN THE TEMPERATURE INCREASES FOR ONE REASON OR ANOTHER.** (We'll only look at heat and light as they are the most important controls...then we'll look at some special situations.)

TAKE NOTE THAT TEMPERATURE IS NORMALLY THE FACTOR THAT PACES THE GROWTH OF PHALS AND POSSIBLY OTHER ORCHIDS AS WELL.

Within limits, the warmer the temperature, the faster the growth rate.

WHEN TEMPS GO UP, INCREASE THE LIGHT LEVEL ALLOWED. WHEN THE LIGHT GOES UP, INCREASE THE TEMPS.

Balance.

This may sound dumb, but you'd be surprised at how many growers raise the temps when the light goes down in the winter and attempt to keep their houses too cool in the bright light of the summer. For example, how do you cope with a long, cool, cloudy spell in the winter? Raise the greenhouse temp a little, right? Wrong!! It should be the *other* way around. Lower it! If you raise the temperature, you'll encourage soft growth that is subject to disease and an easier target for chewing insects.

Higher temperatures need brighter light to sustain healthy, hard growth. When temp goes up, remove shading and raise the light level to match it. Hard tissue is more disease resistant...and vice versa.

IS EVERYONE WITH ME ON THIS? IF NOT, GO BACK AND RE-READ THE LAST COUPLE OF PARAGRAPHS. IT IS VERY IMPORTANT.

When temps go up, water more often. Higher temps mean faster growth and faster water use and loss, so water more frequently. Plants will tolerate higher temps and brighter light with high humidity. As David Grove pointed out in our recent worldwide phal culture survey, higher humidity tends to protect the plants from skyrocketing temperatures on bright days when there is snow on the ground, a problem of some considerable concern to growers in cold country where bright days are common in February, for example. (Are you listening up there in Alberta and Winnipeg?)

Those of you who have visited David Grove's greenhouse may know he is a big believer in humidity. Why not? That's the way it is in the forest where these beauties grow naturally.

To control those temperature spikes, then, increase the humidity and air circulation during the bright hours, but allow an hour or two for the house to air out before the sun goes down. Moisture in the air dampens temperature swings. Where there is high humidity, there is a narrower temperature range between the daytime high and the nighttime low. That's why it stays hot day and night when the humidity is high.

I lived in Toms River, on the New Jersey shore, for 6 years and remember very clearly some soggy mid-summer nights. In fact, I remember a lot of them. High humidity. In dry areas when the sun goes down, the temperature goes down with it...usually. There are exceptions, like Phoenix in mid-summer.

With higher temps *and* brighter light, increase the nitrogen fertilizer. The plant wants to grow; give it the fuel to grow with.

Again, when you increase the light and temperature, increase the air circulation to hold down surface temperature and to avoid hot spots.

You can see we've been around this circle completely, now, but the changes are cyclic, and so should your Yin and Yang adjustments be.

WHEN YOU OR THE WEATHER *LOWERS* THE TEMPERATURE IN THE GREENHOUSE, MAKE THESE ADJUSTMENTS IN REVERSE. WHEN THE TEMPERATURE GOES DOWN, LOWER EVERYTHING ELSE.

IN THE SPRING...INCREASE TEMP, LIGHT, HUMIDITY, WATER, FERTILIZER AND AIR CIRCULATION.

AS A GENERAL RULE, IN THE AUTUMN, DECREASE ALL THOSE THINGS,

but a better rule is to make a point of checking the variables not less often than the first day of each month...every week is better.

Let's look at a few special situations that are not covered by these general rules. I'm going to assume that 'normal' is bright, warm days and cool nights.

In some of these special cases, you will note that the usual rule of balance seems to be violated...and it is. But, these are not cultural conditions which are in harmony to start with. They are problems which are out of balance to begin with and need an out-of-balance solution.

LOW AVERAGE WINTER TEMPERATURES WHICH CANNOT BE RAISED:

What I'm going to suggest is not something you do instead of raising the temperature. This is an expedient only, and should not be used for an extended time.

Increase watering and raise humidity. Plants can tolerate the cold better if they are wet. Add Epsom salts at the rate of 5 teaspoons per gallon to fertilizer. (There are several reports of the Epsom salts helping the phals to tolerate the cold.)

Use Kocide 101 or a systemic bactericide/fungicide at 4-6 week intervals to cope with the increased probability of rot. The increased water and humidity will tend to dampen temperature extremes.

LOW LEVELS OF WINTER LIGHT:

Reduce or discontinue the use of nitrogen fertilizer until flower spikes appear. Lower average temperature a few degrees. Use a bactericide-fungicide such as Kocide 101.

If the low light is a regular thing, consider using metal halide lamps to supplement natural light. Metal halide and high pressure sodium vapor lamps seem to be of about equal value for phals, so buy whichever is cheaper. (Low pressure sodium lamps are somewhat more efficient, but are less available.) Use a reflector for more efficient use. Fluorescents are cheaper for initial investment, but cost more in the long run because the halides are as much as three times more efficient to operate. (Incandescent lamps should not be considered because of the color balance problems and high cost of operation.)

These metal halide lamps are very bright and are available in up to 1,000 watts of illumination. They are still expensive to operate, but will aid in heating the growing area as well. Metal halide lamps are commonly used for warehouse lighting and they make your hands look like you have premature 'liver spots'. High pressure sodium lamps are commonly used for street and parking lot lighting.

A hybrid system of artificial and natural lighting for phal culture in the northern temperate zones...appears to be an idea whose time has come. You may want to think about this if you are a dedicated phal grower in low light country.

LOW WINTER HUMIDITY:

Obviously, water more often, but also slow the air circulation. Keep movement up only enough to keep the air in the greenhouse from settling into layers of warm air up high and cool air down low. "Homogenize" the air, so to speak. Point the fans over or away from the plants.

Increase humidity by misting, too, but use a timer to 'disable' the misting system by noon or early afternoon to give everything a chance to dry out before the sun goes down. Set the timer to 're-enable' the system again about sunup.

Provide a fresh air supply duct from outdoors to the greenhouse heater firebox...if you use one...to avoid losing warm, moist air from your growing area up the stack. Cold air burns the fuel more efficiently than warm air, anyway. Not a bad idea for home heating, either.

HIGH WINTER HUMIDITY:

Increase air circulation; raise temperature; ventilate whenever possible during the day; lengthen the watering interval; use Kocide 101 or any another broad-spectrum antiseptic. (Bordeaux mixture will do if you can't find the Kocide.) If Botrytis becomes a problem, use Benlate or Ornalin fungicides.

HIGH AVERAGE SUMMER TEMPERATURES:

Increase air circulation; reduce the light; increase ventilation; increase watering and humidity; keep the fertilizer up; consider summering out, but remember the rules for growing out-of-doors are the same as those for growing indoors. Run coolers at night to lower respiration and growth rates.

HIGH LEVELS OF SUMMER LIGHT:

Increase air circulation and fertilizer; reduce light by shading; increase water and humidity.

LOW SUMMER HUMIDITY:

Anybody here have this problem? I have it all the time. Slow air circulation; increase water and humidity; if that doesn't work, lower the light and the nitrogen. I know, I know, that will slow the growth down, but something has to give and it is going to have to be the growth rate. No alternatives. Don't worry, you aren't going to lose very much. The plants are likely to be growing at their maximum rate under these conditions, anyway.

Low humidity is tough on seedlings, so consider potting them in a sphagnum medium, such a Fison's Sunshine #1, to keep more moisture around the roots.

HIGH SUMMER HUMIDITY:

Increase air circulation; reduce watering and stop any misting; ventilate when possible; keep up air movement at night; use Kocide 101 or a systemic agent for bacteria and fungi.

HOT DAYS, HOT NIGHTS:

Increase air circulation; run fans on high at night; open doors to ventilate every night; reduce nitrogen to slow growth rate down if new growth is soft.

HOT DAYS, COLD NIGHTS:

Don't you wish!! Use a two-stage thermostat to heat at night and cool during the day; increase nitrogen for fast, solid growth; mist in daytime with a timer to shut off the system in the early afternoon; use Kocide 101 and Dithane to cope with the increased hazard of Pseudomonas and leaf spot.

VERY BRIGHT, BUT COLD WINTER DAYS:

Increase humidity and the air circulation; use Epsom salts with whatever fertilizer you use...if your local water magnesium count is below 15 ppm or if the lab foliar analysis is .8% or lower. Use Kocide 101 to offset bacterial problems; Dithane for fungal problems.

A few years ago, when I was a little concerned with the quality of the local water supply and, especially, about total dissolved salts or TDS, I sent a sample off to a state lab to be analyzed. A few weeks later, the county agent who handled it for me called to say the results were back. When I asked about the TDS, he said "I don't know anything about that, but the guy at the state lab said to tell you he thinks your horse has diabetes." You think *you* have bad water!

ARTIFICIAL LIGHTING:

Because most artificial light growers don't have these extreme conditions to contend with, there aren't too many situations for them out of the ordinary. Artificial light culture is, by nature, a stable process. But, there are changes necessary to fooling the plant into thinking it is still out in the forest, and getting it to bloom.

Keep pace, under the lights, with outdoor weather changes by shortening the 'day' length gradually down to about 9 hours or so on the shortest day of the year...and lengthening to 12-14 hours on the longest day of the year. Regular, small adjustments are in order.

Chances are, you won't have to make any deliberate adjustments downward on room temperature, because indoor changes will reflect more or less what's going on outside.

Make the other adjustments that sunlight growers do to water, humidity, fertilizer, Epsom salts and air circulation.

Recommended: draw up a personal culture plan and commit it to writing; ask the society experts to put together a culture plan for the most popular genera and publish it in your society's bulletin; the alternative is to continue making the same mistakes year after year...without knowing why. Give the society new guys the benefit of your experience.

A plan or a journal or a log is the difference in a grower having, say, 10 years experience one year at a time and having the same one year's experience ten times. We've all met both kinds. And there's a lot of difference!

OTHER:

There are other adjustments we can make to tailor phal culture to our personal needs and habits. For example, if you like to water, use a more open or coarse potting medium. You can also increase the amount of pot drainage by making more or larger holes.

If you don't like to water a lot or don't have the time, use a finer mix for potting...or use New Zealand moss.

If you don't have time to repot every year, sift the bark you use and soak it overnight. Use only the stuff that floats.

In closing this section, once each week, make adjustments for the seasonal changes that have happened in the past week. This is the price we pay for growing phals and not living in an area where these honeys grow naturally.

As with Yin and Yang, we adjust to maintain a sameness; we do it in our own lives when we put on winter clothing when it gets cold and sun glasses when it is too bright outside. That's not doing much for evolutionary progress of the plants, but that isn't our goal, either.

Section 15. HYBRIDIZING.

When you get the urge to make your own Phalaenopsis hybrids, the time has come for a little peek into your motives for wanting to do so. That sounds pretty heavy, but a little chat is in order, because the truth is that here, as in other circumstances, a privilege carries a responsibility. (Why, all of a sudden, do I feel like I'm talking to one of my kids about sex?)

If you want to pollinate a flower just for the hell of it, fine, have at it. See how the wonderful mechanism works; it is an awesome experience and the heady prospect of controlling life never fades for some of us. It's like pressing the 'push to test' button on a process that has taken thousands or even millions of years to evolve.

And you can invoke these marvels of nature with a toothpick.

But you can also saddle the orchid-growing community with a batch of trash plants in your exuberance if your choice of parents is not deliberately and thoughtfully planned. We once had a barn cat that had kittens every time she could. *She* didn't have much choice, but, hopefully, we will not exercise a privilege just because we can. We can advance orchidology...or we can set it back.

The Deity blessed us with the ability to reason, so let us reason before we pollinate. To do less is a disservice to ourselves and to the rest of the orchid world.

Crosses made for the express purpose of 'seeing if it works' are okay with orchid growers everywhere IF you have them flasked, replated, and raise them to flowering yourself and

IF you keep all of them to yourself. The big condition is that you don't release them to the public. Flower them, and if they turn out to be mediocre, trash-can them.

We are up to our belly buttons in junk crosses now and not all of those are made by hobbyists, incidentally. I know that smacks of genocide, but it's irrational to think that everything we do should be preserved for posterity. Practice a little, and throw away your failures. When you have something really good to offer the world, make it something you will be proud of.

I'm getting around to saying

IT IS IMPORTANT THAT YOU HAVE A SPECIFIC GOAL IN MIND WHEN YOU MAKE A CROSS.

Write that purpose down...I mean with pen and notebook; when you log the cross in some sort of a record, write down why you made the cross and what you hope to achieve by doing it. You will learn from your mistakes this way...and you will force yourself to think things through before acting; a good idea anytime.

Are you trying for something bigger, rounder, better-colored, with splashes, smaller, more floriferous, or what? What you are looking for is your business, but put the purpose of the cross in writing. How will you know if you succeeded or failed otherwise? A number of years back and after then 40-some years in orchids, Ernest Hetherington advised new hybridizers to (1) buy the best stud plants they could afford; (2) hybridize with them only and; (3) learn all they could about those studs e.g. what qualities do these produce that are dominant? How do they react when crossed to a particular type of other breeder? What can the progeny be expected to look like? I asked Ernest at the time how many stud plants he thought he knew well, expecting an answer in the 300-500 range. He said "Ten".

It just takes a long time to learn because most phal generations are 3 to 4 years long. That's short. The cattleyas take 5 to 7 years and catts are what Ernest was talking about. His point was well made.

I think we can expect soon to see computer analyses and projections replacing the 40-50 years of hybridizing wisdom that Ernest, Herb Hager, Charley Beard, Roy Fukumura, Henry Wallbrun, W.G.G. Moir, Hugo Freed, Bill Kirsch, John Miller, Maurice LeCoufle, Amado Vasquez and a few others have or had...but never completely. Dr. Joe Arditti put it as well as anyone when he said "Hybridizing is not a science; it is an art."

I'd like to add a few thoughts on responsible hybridizing: Decide what you are after; ask for advice on your ideas from those whose opinions you respect and who have been at it for a while; hold off till you can get what you think is the best available parent to get the job done; make the cross and HOLD ON TO ALL THE PROGENY. Then flower them and draw some specific conclusions about what you have done. If they are good, share them with others. If not, you know where and nowhere else!

I'm asking nothing more than responsible parenthood.

Knowing specifically what you are after is not a quick and easy step. It requires that you make some decisions regarding your future in orchids. If it is just to grow and enjoy, forget about hybridizing. If you want to go on, decide what is your niche in the orchid world. Marketing managers call this segmenting the market; a fitting analogy since you may want to become THE SOURCE of a particular type of plant.

Decide where you want to fit in. Do you want to change the course of Phalaenopsis breeding in the world? If so, with what color? Are you headed up or down in size?

Herb Hager, 10 years ago and after 50-some years in orchids decided to breed for what he called 'square Phalaenopsis'. Marvelous! You'll find people around who are looking to breed red, green, blue, square, fragrant, cold resistant, smog resistant, miniatures, and on and on.

PICK OUT WHAT IS FOR YOU. Become a specialist and stick to it, if that pleases you, but **KNOW WHERE YOU ARE GOING.**

It's hard to get anywhere otherwise. One wit said if you don't know where you're going, at least you're never lost. Maybe so, but a clear goal in mind makes life much simpler.

Personally, I have in mind to produce a 5-inch, emerald-green Phalaenopsis...then one with red stripes. I'm in no hurry and I know where I'm going. That's a nice, comfortable feeling. How far I get doesn't mean a whit to the world, but my life is meaningful and holds the tantalizing promise of changing Something and making the world a nicer place to live in. (God, I love that kind of talk.)

If you think *I'm* bananas, I won't tell you that my wife, Nancy, is trying to make a *blue* Phalaenopsis! I hope no one tells her she can't. People who say something can't be done shouldn't get in the way of those who are doing it.

135

BREEDING PHILOSOPHY.

Herb Hager, one of America's modern orchid pioneers, gave a talk on Phalaenopsis breeding at the 11th World Orchid Conference in Miami in March 1984. (The text appears in the Proceedings of the 11th WOC) Two points he made that stuck with me and make a lot of sense with regard to phals:

(1) SELF-POLLINATE A PLANT TO GET A COMPLETE SPECTRUM OF WHAT QUALITIES THAT CLONE HAS TO OFFER (DISPERSE) AND (2) SIBLING-CROSS TO CONCENTRATE A DESIRED QUALITY THAT BOTH SIBS HAVE (FOCUS).

He does this in alternate generations to progressively concentrate the characteristics he's looking for. (If you laughed when I said earlier Herb had said some years ago he wanted to make a 'square' phal, you may want to reconsider his chances of success.)

Okay, if you are still with me on the hybridizing thing, let's run through a little exercise in personal-direction development:

1. WHAT DO YOU WANT TO DO?
(Write it down)

2. WHY DO YOU WANT TO DO THAT?
(Write it down)

3. WHO CAN HELP?
(Make a list)

4. HOW DO YOU PROPOSE TO START?
(Write it down)

5. WHEN ARE YOU GOING TO DO IT?
(Make a schedule)

6. WHAT ARE YOU WAITING FOR?
(Get up and do it)

I don't want to take the fun out of a little sex-in-the-greenhouse, but think of hybridizing as a trip somewhere. Would you go without a map, gas, clothes, money...or a destination? Good. Having thought about that, let's get into how it all happens.

Section 14.1 THE MECHANICS OF HYBRIDIZING.

Phalaenopsis plants can be self-pollinated (selfed), cross-pollinated with other Phalaenopsis (many will; at least some reject parenthood), and cross-pollinated with at least 15 other species and 25 intergeneric hybrids of the vandaceous group. So, you have a lot of material to work with.

Some of the crosses (read: hybrids) are pretty far out and unlikely to have occurred in nature; for example, the Phalaenopsis that is native to the southwest Pacific and southeast Asia can be cross-bred with the genus eurychone, a native of Uganda in Africa. (admittedly, a difficult cross, but it has been done)

Since the 'male' and 'female' parts of the flower are located on the same member and are quite close together, better go get your glasses before we start. (I hope no one picks up this book and starts reading here; this is good, clean fun, folks, honest!)

On the projection from the center of the flower, which is called the column, the tip houses the pollen, the boy part. On the under side and immediately behind the pollen 'cap' is an oval depressed area with a shiny, sticky surface. This is the 'girl' part or stigma, sometimes called the stigmatic surface. When you've looked at one and seen how small they are, you'll see why I sent you for your glasses.

To remove pollen in preparation for pollination: Cup one hand under the pollen-donor flower and, with a toothpick, ease the pollen cap off the column. It helps to break off the lip of the flower before starting this process; it gets in the way. In fact, I always remove the lip so I won't have any trouble telling which flower I pollinated when I turn away to make a tag to record the event. Take off the petals and sepals, too, if it makes the job any easier. The flower won't need them any longer. Their function was to attract a pollinator...and they did...you!

You'll only flip a few pollen caps off before you find what the cupped hand under the flower is for. It's to catch the 'fliers'.

Press the end of the toothpick onto the sticky pad that is on the end of the little tail (the caudicle) that projects down and under the column and remove the pollen cap and the pollen.

Holding the toothpick with one hand, with the fingernails of the other hand, pull the cap off the pair of pollinia. Dispose of the cap. It, too, has done its job. You'll be left with a toothpick with two, little oval-shaped, gold-or lavender-colored packets called pollinia. (actually, they are many little grains of pollen held together by a waxy substance.)

You can pollinate a Phalaenopsis with either or both of these. Some hybridizers will cut a scarce pollen packet into several pieces and pollinate separate flowers with each piece. Steve Pridgen, a surgeon, who knows a thing or two about handling such delicate things,

advises using 2-diamond forceps for handling pollen...and swears by them. He gave me a couple of pair of the forceps and I've become a convert. Caution, though. The sharp points of the forceps or tweezers can puncture the skin of the stigma and could transfer a virus if present on the tips. The dull end of a toothpick does not present that hazard... except to heavy-handed klutz' like some of us.

As a matter of practice, remove the pollen from a flower to be pollinated. Dispose of it if it is not to be used elsewhere. It isn't likely to cause problems if left in, but it could.

To consummate the union, dip the dull end of the toothpick or forceps into the sticky substance in the stigma (it's called honey, because that's what it tastes like) and pick up the pollen with the sticky end. The stigmatic surface is a shallow, bowl-shaped cup under the column and behind the void left where you removed the pollen or pollen (anther) cap. I usually wet the end of the toothpick on the tip of my tongue to ensure a good grip on the pollen.

Press the pollen gently into the honey, preferably at the *back* of the stigma and smear honey over the pollen. This placement at the back of the stigma shortens the distance that the little pollen tubes which sprout from the pollen have to travel to make a score. Sometimes they don't make the distance because their little tubes are too short and can't reach the ovary section of the flower. (Why, all of a sudden, do I think I'm talking to my kids about sex again) And, that's it. It's done.

When you place the pollinia onto the stigmatic surface, take care not to poke too hard with the toothpick. You could damage the surface

137

and, if by chance the pollen should be virused, infect the host parent. If no damage is done to the stigma, even if the pollen is virused, it is unlikely to pass the problem on to the host parent.

A lot has to happen before seed is developed, but, you're finished with your part. Now the waiting begins.

The 'take' rate of crosses made with like-size, like-color, and like-species usually are fairly high. Fifty percent is a good average. Some of these that 'take' initially will abort before full term. Some of those that go full term will produce only a few or no viable seed, that is, seed capable of coming to life.

The success rate goes down as you depart from conventional crosses to the more exotic ones. Between 5 and 10 percent of my green phal cross attempts (admittedly novel) actually produce good seed. Nancy's attempts at blue phal crosses are even less successful. The rate is much higher with big pinks or big whites.

A general rule is to put the pollen of the larger of the two flowers on the stigma of the smaller, but that only satisfies a mechanical need. There are all manner of reasons why the cross should be made in the other direction, but they have to do with genetics, not physiology.

At times some clones or individuals will only act as a 'pollen parent' and sometimes only as a 'pod parent', and other times they will function as either. To further muddy this fertility business, some clones must go through a period of puberty before they will assume the responsibilities of parenthood. Seriously!

Full term on most phal crosses is 4 to 5 months, for full maturity of the seed capsule. If the capsule is to be sown in a 'green pod' condition, it can be done as early as 110 days, but better to leave it to 120. Difficult crosses should be left upwards of 180 to 190 days, in order to give the plant time to make good seed. Violacea crosses are among those that profit from long development times.

Yellowing of the seed capsule usually indicates an imminent change of status, such as abort or capsule ripening. If it turns yellow and splits before 90 days, it probably is fruitless (no pun intended) to flask it. It is doubtful with most phal species backgrounds that there will be any good seed.

If you have a seed-sowing lab close by, you are a little safer in letting the capsule go to full term, but not much. Ripening of the capsule happens sometimes in as little as 12 to 36 hours, after which it splits, necessitating a more complicated flasking process which involves sterilizing the seed. Sterilization of the seed is not necessary if the capsule is flasked in the 'green pod' condition. Seed is sometimes damaged in the sterilization process; sometimes all the seed dies as a result.

Roy Fukumura (another of the Great Older Guys in Phals) suggests pouring seed from a split capsule into a test tube and shaking with common hydrogen peroxide for 45 seconds then pouring it all out into a sterile flask with germinating media. Save unused seed in sterile paper in a refrigerator.

If the capsule has or is about to split in a given area, flame the area with an alcohol lamp before sowing and use only the seed *away* from the split area. Without a magnifying glass it is hard to tell just when the capsule begins to split and when the contamination enters.

So, you're boxed in by (1) the need to go as long as possible to ensure good seed and (2) the knowledge that the capsule may ripen and split (contaminating the seed) before you get it flasked. You are probably safe in harvesting most phal seed capsules at 120 to 130 days after pollination and 'green pod' flasking them.

If you want lots and lots of seedlings, as is the case with most commercial hybridizers, take a chance and go longer. More mature seed is dryer and easier to spread in the flask, incidentally, and avoids the clumping which makes re-flasking difficult.

To remove a seed capsule, sterilize a pair of shears and snip it off. If you're mailing it to a lab, wrap it in tissue or typing paper, never plastic. Mold can form while in transit and damage the capsule. If it has split, carefully shake the dry seed onto a piece of typing paper and throw the dried seed capsule away. Don't send it with the seed. It can carry and cause fungal growth in the seeds.

Mark the capsule with your name, your registration number, (assign one) and the species of the cross (phal). The flasker will need that information. Ship it off, invoke the fertility gods and wait to see if you fired a good shot or a blank one.

Some growers I know go to elaborate security measures to make sure the lab folks don't find out what their cross is and steal their great stuff...but you really needn't worry. I've never run across one who was even the slightest bit interested. I have also known some of these paranoid growers who, after taking

elaborate security measures, lost the key to their code...and the identity of the cross.

Most Phalaenopsis crosses will germinate within 3 to 4 months, if they're going to germinate at all. I've had germination begin at 16 months after flasking, long after the bottle should have been emptied out and washed. Germination is usually quicker if the capsule has gone full term and commensurately slower if taken early. Usually a lab will send you a postcard when germination has occurred and ask how many 're-plates' you want from the cross.

A re-plate is a flask with a stronger nutrient formula, into which embryos from the mother or seed flask are sown. Seedlings from a re-plate can usually be taken from the bottle and sown in a community pot...without any further laboratory activity.

If you are doing your own flasking, and there is little reason not to if you are interested, keep the flasks warm...75-80°F...and they will germinate and grow quicker than if kept cool and seedlings grown quicker do better after being potted out. Seedlings that have been in a bottle a long time usually don't grow well after being removed.

Growth in the re-plate flask is quicker and seedlings will grow much larger than they would if left in the mother flask. Mother flasks get very crowded if germination rate is high and the embryos will grow to a certain size and stop... as if in suspended animation until they are reflasked with more room and a diet more suitable for a robust seedling.

Seed or mother flask nutrients are made quite 'mild' to accommodate the needs of germinating seeds.

Like baby food or formula.

In dry environments like ours locally, you may have to add sterile water to the flasks every few months to compensate for evaporation through the breathing hole in the flask. Even those seedlings grown 'anaerobically', with sealed tops and no air exchange, need the additional water in a dry climate. Add sterilized water under sterile conditions, just like when sowing the seed.

Water can be sterilized by boiling in a pressure cooker at 15 pounds per square inch for 15 minutes. Leave the top loose during the heating and tighten it as soon as the bottle can be removed from the pressure cooker safely. Leather work or garden gloves are required for handling hot bottles!

Seed sowing labs will have a charge to flask a seed pod, whether it germinates or not. It's the same amount of work and expense for them. Another charge is levied for each 're-plate' flask you order. There are anywhere from 15-50 seedlings in a re-plate flask, depending on flask size and the lab's policy.

Too many seedlings in a flask is bad news. They will consume the water and nutrients before they're big enough to make it on their own in the Real World. Then you're faced with the prospect of another round of re-plating (and costs) or trying to get the little dudes to make it in a community pot, a sad mistake.

They pot out seedlings only one-half inch in leaf span in Hawaii, but their growing conditions are near perfect and they get a lot of practice at it and have an understanding of how to cope with the special problems associated with early potting out. Don't be tempted. It's usually a waste of time and the seedlings

will probably die in the end anyway. Don't try to remove them before they're an inch in leaf span or larger.

Twenty-five seedlings are comfortable in a 500 ml (about a pint) bottle. Flaskers aren't doing you any favors by putting in more than that. If they do it, find another lab.

REGISTRATION OF NEW HYBRIDS.

Names of crosses that have merit and represent a contribution to the orchid world should be registered with the Royal Horticultural Society in London. The American Orchid Society requires registration of all plants selected by AOS judges for awards.

If a clone of an un-named cross is selected for an award by the AOS, announcement is withheld until the registration appears in the *Orchid Review,* a British publication which makes first public notice of newly registered hybrids. If the hybrid, or cross, is not registered in a year or so, the award is canceled.

Registration is simple and relatively inexpensive. Contact the American Orchid Society, 6000 S. Olive Ave., West Palm Beach, Florida 33405 for guidance and forms.

Unhappily, in recent years the orchid hybrid registration lists have been used by some commercial nurseries as a source of cheap advertising by incorporating the nursery's name in the hybrid's registered name...and the practice is growing. The ploy is a shabby imposition on orchid growers worldwide and should be discouraged. I, for one, would be delighted to see the RHS take a firm stand on this issue.

(Even sadder to relate is that, since I wrote the paragraph above in 1985, the practice of working nursery names into registered names has become even more widespread and even more obnoxious. Such perversion of an otherwise useful medium for the systematic identification of orchid hybrids would make Linnaeus turn over in his grave. The practitioners who do it and those who condone it should hang their collective heads in shame.)

I believe the RHS could stop it by refusing to accept a second hybrid name with such a preface or, minimally, using a nursery name as part of a hybrid name only once; and thereafter use only the nursery initials. They might also triple the fee for such registrations and call it a value-added tax. But then, nurseries pay a lot of registration fees...

Am I the only grower in the world who finds this practice contemptible?

Section 16. SHOW PREPARATION

PREPARATION OF PHALAENOPSIS FOR SHOW, WITH OR WITHOUT JUDGING, BEGINS AT LEAST ONE YEAR OR ONE FULL GROWING SEASON BEFORE THE PLANT IS TO BE PRESENTED TO THE VIEWING PUBLIC.

The elements of good Phalaenopsis culture detailed above are the basis of good show preparation, because good health is essential if a plant's good qualities are to be peaked for the showing. A sick or weak plant cannot score well any more than a sick athlete can perform well in competition. Robust health allows a plant's best qualities to be seen in the most favorable light.

GOOD PLANT HEALTH IS THE FIRST STEP IN SHOW PREPARATION.

Few plants shown to the public or AOS judges or both get the kind of attention I'm going to suggest, but attention to these details will maximize your chances of presenting a plant at the very best appearance it is capable of. This is what orchid culture is all about. It's what we work so hard for. There's not much joy in having something beautiful if you can't share it with others. The quality of its presentation to the public will be a product of the plant's genes and your efforts. Both are needed.

Okay, most of our specific show preparations are going to begin at 3 to 4 months before the plant reaches its flowering peak. For most spring-blooming phals, this is early autumn and back a little we talked about setting the spikes during this time. It gets busy with other things about then, so try to do your re-potting earlier, say during early summer, June and July in the northern hemisphere.

There are going to be many that don't bloom then, especially the summer bloomers like amboinensis and violacea which peak June-August. Repot these plants in December through February.

IF YOU HAVE PLANTS THAT ARE DUE REPOTTING DURING THE BLOOMING SEASON, DO IT 5 TO 6 MONTHS BEFOREHAND

and give them time to get over the trauma before settling down to the business of flowering.

Don't do them during or just before blooming; they're too busy getting beautiful.

There shouldn't be many times when you *must* repot just before flowering, but if there are, follow these rules:

Mix a little of the old media in with the new after sterilizing it. Handle the plant gently and don't cut any roots. Use a slightly over-sized pot and take the time to stuff all the roots in and don't allow any out the drain holes. Don't cut any roots. Picky? Sure it is, but why allow something that will detract the viewer's attention from the beauty of the flower. Drench the roots with a solution of vitamin B-1 (available in any gardening shop) or use SuperThrive. Water the plant a bit more often than you would one potted on the regular schedule. Spritzing for a week or 10 days after repotting is a good idea, too.

As a temporary fix, you could also put the whole plant, pot and all, in a larger pot, filling in all the spaces with new bark. Then do the regular repotting after the show.

Back to our show preparation: 3-4 months before blooming,

PLACE THE PLANT, WITH ITS BEST PRESENTATION OF LEAVES FACING TO THE LIGHT SOURCE.

If you grow under lights, place the plant slightly away from the lamp tubes with its best presentation of leaves facing the light. To find a plant's best face, set it before you and rotate it slowly until its array of leaves looks the most attractive. This is the side that should face the light. The flower spike will try to look in the same direction, so both flowers and leaves will show their best face on this side.

It follows that this is the face you will offer to the public or the judges later on. The judges, of course, will look at *all* sides, but chances are good their opinions will be formed while looking at its best side. True, judges need not consider leaf appearance in point scoring, but a pleasing appearance will not go unnoticed.

If the flower spike gets too long to handle when you grow under fluorescent lamps, move it to a windowsill to finish blooming or rig a metal halide lamp over a 'finishing bench' to complete the job. The metal halides are much more powerful light producers and a 1,000 watt unit can be suspended 5 or even 6 feet above the plant. Then the plant can finish developing its flower spike normally.

I met a grower in Montreal, Quebec, who brought two huge, beautiful blue vandas to a society meeting in November. I asked if he had just brought them from Hawaii or Florida and he answered, "No, I grew them here in Montreal." When I looked shocked, he told me he grew them under metal halide lamps, 1,000-watt units, two of them...one for each vanda. Cheap hydro-electric power is the best-kept secret in Canada.

Having selected the plant's best angle and put it facing the light (south usually),

LEAVE THE POT UNDISTURBED UNTIL THE PLANT FLOWERS.

This way ensures a single, unbroken, graceful arch in the formation of the spike which, in large measure, is the basis of the plant's 'carriage'...if the plant is capable of producing one. Not all Phalaenopsis plants have good, natural carriage, but a single-arc flower spike will improve even the worst looking plant. Moving the plant to a different orientation during spike formation will not deter it from seeking the sun, even if it has to twist and turn several times to do it. The result is a crooked spike. So, once having set the plant in its proper orientation, leave it there.

DON'T TRY TO BEND OR SHAPE A HARDENED SPIKE. IT WILL BREAK.

Stake and tie the spike at about the first flowering node above pot level. That's the fifth node up from the bottom on most phals. It's higher on the tall, skinny ones. Secure the spike to the stake loosely or use a stake with a U-shaped top to cradle it. To make that work, cut the stake to the approximate length needed. You may have to bend or move the stake slightly to keep the spike coming in the best perspective. Usually this means moving the suspension point up or back a bit to compensate for the additional weight of the spike as it grows.

143

A NIE-CO-ROL inertia reel is especially useful for this purpose, because it moves and readjusts continuously as the spike grows. I've seen all manner of set-ups to keep a gently, constant tension on flower spikes, all of which seemed to work well. This is a challenge to the gadgeteers among the readers.

When the lower half of the spike hardens, remove the stake or NIE-CO-ROL and experiment with a point where the support will be placed during flowering. This usually will be lower than the point where you supported it during spike development and is especially true of the big plant spikes which are long enough to take on the familiar cascade for which Phalaenopsis is so well known. If this is your objective,

THE 'BOTTOM' FLOWER ON THE SPIKE WILL BE AT THE HIGHEST POINT ON THE ARC AND THE 'TOP' FLOWER WILL BE AT THE LOWEST. CAN YOU PICTURE THAT?

Allow for the extra weight that the spike will gain as the flowers mature and open. You may have to move the support point several times as the spike matures.

GROOMING, OR THE PRACTICE OF ARTIFICIALLY MANIPULATING THE SHAPE OF A PLANT, FLOWER SPIKE OR FLOWER DURING DEVELOPMENT, IS PROHIBITED ON PLANTS ENTERED INTO AMERICAN ORCHID SOCIETY JUDGING.

It *is* done, however, but for personal gain of the grower and not for the good of the orchid world. For the most part, orchid growers are a notch above the average conscience in our society and playing fair is part of the game ...usually.

The staking routine described above is permissible, and in fact, is expected.

Be especially careful not to splash cold water on the newly developing flower spike. Mesophyll tissue collapse or thermal shock, technically, only occurs in plant leaf tissue, but the collapse in flower spikes is quite similar and is caused, also, by application of cold water on tender, new plant tissue. New flower buds respond by dying.

As flower buds begin to differentiate or take form, **SWITCH FERTILIZER BACK FROM HIGH PHOSPHORUS TO A BALANCED FORMULA.**

We want the nitrogen now to pump everything up in size. Increase the frequency of watering. Keep these show plants a little more moist than the others, but increase use of Physan, too, because the danger of bacterial rot increases with increased moisture.

Look closely at your plants frequently for insect presence and damage. The scars will still be there when the plant is shown and they are distracting, to say the least.

AS THE FIRST BUDS APPROACH OPENING, MOVE THE PLANT INTO LOWER LIGHT (800-900 fc),

keeping the same orientation to the light. The lower light and cooler temperatures will allow a more lush, softer and larger development of the blooms that is the hallmark of cultured plants. It's probably getting close to the time to increase shading on your greenhouse or growing area, too.

We're getting close, now, and hopefully the flowering date is going to coincide with the show date. Cooler temperatures will slow flowering a little and, conversely, increasing light and temperature will speed it a bit, but not much. Raising minimum temperatures at night to 68°F. will help speed things up. Fortunately, phals will stay in show condition a lot longer than most orchids, so better you should be opening the flowers early than late.

A day or so before the show, clean the leaves and spikes to remove dust, dirt and water marks. A wipe-down with a tissue and full-fat milk will put a nice gloss on the leaves and show them at their best. Use commercial leaf shining materials at your peril. They can put an unnatural gloss on plants that turns some people off, including judges. Better stay safe and use milk. Lemon juice in a little water helps clean the surfaces and is quite good on water stains. Use a Q-tip to clean the hard-to-get spots and don't forget the flower stems.

Shine up the pot, too. Secure ties on the stake and add some if the spike is floppy, but be careful not to induce an unnatural angle to the flowers. Extra ties are in order to avoid damage in transit to the show. Remove the extra staking just before show time. Of course, protect the spike from wind and sun damage in transit. Water the plant one last time the day before leaving for the show.

It almost goes without saying, that a plant suspected of being diseased or infested should never be brought among other plants at a show. Beside incurring the wrath of the other exhibitors, the plant will probably be thrown out by the judges, anyway. They aren't dummies; most are pretty savvy, have been around orchids a long time, and know what a sick plant looks like and, also, how quickly a sick or infested plant can spread its problem to other plants there. If you don't want to be

treated like something that just crawled out from under a rock, keep your sick or buggy plants at home where they belong.

Having done all of the above, be assured you have controlled what can be controlled. The rest is up to the plant and the judges. Good luck.

Section 17. WHAT KIND TO GROW?
(Pick a color, any color.)

DON'T YOU DARE SKIP THIS SEC-TION! THERE'S STUFF IN HERE FOR ALL PHAL GROWERS, INCLUDING THOSE WHO HAVE ALREADY DECID-ED WHAT KIND TO GROW.

Rather than just stumbling into growing what-ever you have most of in your greenhouse the way most of us do, it can be useful to think a little before you start or, as is more probably the case, to organize your thinking and reorga-nize how you go about growing your orchids.

It is common practice in the business world to sit down periodically and ask or re-ask the pur-pose of the enterprise; then set down the answer to the question in writing...to serve as a guide in future business activities as a charter. The prac-tice works with people's activities, too. It doesn't have to be like drawing up articles of incorporation, only to ask yourself "what do I get the most enjoyment or reward from?"

Sometimes, the answers will knock your socks off because they aren't what you may have assumed before. Knowing what does the most for you, you can concentrate on those things and maximize your enjoyment and eliminate the confusion that results from try-ing to learn about all the 700 plus orchid species and 75,000 or so hybrids (that have been registered).

PICK ONE SPECIES, OR PICK JUST SPECIES, AND LEARN ALL YOU CAN ABOUT IT...AND WATCH THE CONFU-SION AND FEAR OF NOT KNOWING WHAT YOU ARE DOING...DRAIN AWAY. PHALS ARE A GOOD CHOICE.

In the vernacular, phals are 'user-friendly' and a great place to begin really enjoying the world's most sophisticated flower. Let's take a look at the different groups of people who grow them. Maybe you'll see yourself here.

I've noted five different groupings of Phalaenopsis enthusiasts; there may be many more, but these represent the majority of the different types of growers I've met. In a descending order of number of fans:

GROWERS: FOR THE FUN AND PRET-TIES.

Far and away the largest group of phal grow-ers is in this category. They grow phals, prob-ably along with other orchids just for the pure enjoyment of the classical elegance of the flowers and in the company of others who do the same. (Included are those who won a few phals from the plant raffle table and don't want to throw them away.)

Most of this group are very sociable and enjoy flower shows, field trips, and other orchid society activities. Many of this group don't have greenhouses, not at this stage at least, and grow their phals as super house plants. For these folks, I recommend a selection of small whites and pinks, a few novelties and a few species Phalaenopsis, the numbers depending on space available.

Large whites and pinks take up a lot of room; as much as, if not more than, a large cattleya. Avoid phals mounted on slabs if you don't have a greenhouse. (Even if you *have* a green-house, avoid them.) They need to be watered at least once a day in the dry weather and that can be a nuisance even with a greenhouse, but more so in the home. You can learn to hate a plant like that.

146

THERE REALLY IS NO REASON NOT TO GROW A LITTLE OF EVERYTHING IN THE PHALAENOPSIS GENUS IF YOU ARE IN THIS GROUP.

This grouping of growers is a first stage for many who later on become serious growers in one of the other categories of enthusiasts. About all you have to *avoid* is getting more than you can handle, especially the big whites and pinks.

How big the plants are going to be when they mature is hard to know when they're in two and a half-inch pots, so ask about the mature size of the plant when buying. Even better, buy them in flower, but that's no guarantee, either. I bought a modest-sized angraecum sesquipedale in flower and several years later had to make a decision between getting rid of it or building it a greenhouse of its own. I put the varietal name 'Fat Albert' on it. Guess why.

Size of the plant and tight space limitations make a pretty good case for considering miniature phals. Interest in Phalaenopsis minis has caught up with that of the cattleya minis, and shortly will surpass them.

We're starting to see more of the lindenii, javanica, parishii, and equestris hybrids now and some of these are true miniatures, with a leaf span of only 8 to 10 inches on a mature plant and clouds of lovely, little flowers on spikes only 8 inches in length.

Collecting and growing these tiny beauties could be an enchanting experience and, it follows, that hybridizing them may be an exciting ride on the wave of the future of Phalaenopsis orchids.

Want to make a mark in the history books? Look no further than right here. The miniature oncidiums and cattleyas certainly are being grown in numbers that few outside of people like Jack Woltmon and Frank Fordyce would have thought possible just a few years ago. I think that these would be a practical and pleasant choice of phals to grow in the cooler regions.

In shopping for the little growers like these, watch and ask for crosses made with equestris, javanica, parishii, and lindenii, particularly among themselves. Phal Cassandra (equestris x stuartiana) is another excellent mini-breeder.

Should you decide to specialize in miniature phals, I think you will find the field wide open and it won't take most thinking people long to get to the threshold of the art.

SOME OF THE GROUPINGS IN ORCHIDS ARE OVER-POPULATED, SO IF YOU LIKE A LOT OF COMPANY, STAY WITH THE GENERALISTS. BUT IF YOU LIKE THE IDEA OF DOING SOMETHING NO ONE HAS DONE BEFORE YOU, BECOME A SPECIALIST.

If you do, you will find very quickly how relatively little is known about Phalaenopsis hybridizing by the world and just how wide open a field it is. To dabble...or dive in; that's a good question, the answer to which is, probably, yes.

GROWERS: THE SERIOUS HOBBYIST AND AMATEUR HYBRIDIZER.

This second largest group of phal growers probably represents no more than 5 per cent of orchid growers in general. Most arrived in this group by way of the above one, and are mostly people who enjoy a challenge or doing something uncommon or useful to society. The idea of putting their names in a history book is usually buried not too deeply. They are the phal nuts, the evangelists, the bores who see life in terms of how it affects the Phalaenopsis genus, who write books on them, and who walk around with silly smiles on their faces as though they'd just discovered the Meaning of Life (and they may have).

If escape from boredom and tedium is among your reasons for growing orchids in general or phals in particular, I invite you to join us; this way to the deep end.

There are many reasons why people become serious phal growers. Some see commercial possibilities, or self-realization, or glamour in association with a symbol of elegance or the multitude of other reasons why people do as they do. The self-satisfaction and feeling of well-being enjoyed by these enthusiasts usually falls only to researchers, scientists and educators. Headiness takes on a new dimension when you've experienced the highs enjoyed by these committed amateurs.

Members of this group also are a major source of forward movement in orchidology because they have the time, the means and incentive to do things that are not yet done, especially those things that do not promise monetary reward...at least not right away.

Among this group is a greater degree of specialization than in other groups because it quickly becomes apparent to them that limitation of subject material is necessary before any progress can be made. You have to find a hand-hold on the elephant before you can pick him up.

You will find here specialists in yellow, red, green, orange, and even blue. Some are working on miniatures, multifloras, cold-resistant, smog-resistant, square-flowered, fragrance, intergeneric hybrids, splash petals, albinos, whites with colored lips and other such tasty subjects that intrigue the inquisitive mind. If you see yourself in the group, come join. You might even join John Miller, Dr. Steve Pridgen, me and a few others in the search for the Perfect Green.

A FEW ARE SUCCESSFUL AT GROWING PHALS COMMERCIALLY,

but not many. Marketing outlets are limited, fickle, and saturated with lower-priced products that compete for discretionary dollars. One major nursery owner told me the only reason why he continued in the business was the appreciation of the market value of greenhouse real estate. There is, however, a very substantial number of hobbyists and fun-growers who sell a few plants and flowers and subsidize their 'habit' this way.

If you have in mind to grow phals for profit, be advised that the principal market is flowering plants; pinks, whites and stripes; and essentially limited to the months of February through May. These are mostly sold to non-orchidists and concentrated around the holidays of Valentines Day, Easter and Mothers Day. The sale of phals to orchid growers is fairly constant throughout the year, but heaviest in the spring when Phalaenopsis flowers are in bloom.

A sad aspect of 'going commercial' on a significant scale, though, is the compromising of amateur ideals in the process. It is very difficult, if not impossible, to do both. You may find it less than gratifying to pursue this course, because you will find yourself grow-ing things that the market wants...and not what you want. Are you ready for that?

Before you take the step, or make any serious commitment to do so, talk to local hobbyists or commercial growers about the market. It is highly segmented, seasonal, and small.

Disappointed? Good. I may just have saved you a lot of money and heartache.

GROWERS: AND THEN THERE ARE THE SPECIES NUTS.

Among the most highly-motivated idealists in Phalaenopsis culture are those who focus their attention on the species of one or more genera and whose objective is the preservation of all existing orchid species, with special attention to those in danger of extinction.

Their methods of preservation range from propagation of rare species to the establish-ment of seed banks where seed and pollen are stored cryogenically for the future. A fasci-nating appeal for the need to preserve the endangered species, including orchids, appears in a book Plant Extinction: a Global Crisis by Dr. Harold Koopowitz of UC Irvine, himself an AOS judge, an orchid enthusiast and a guru of the conservation movement. Highly recommended reading. (Koopowitz and Kaye,1983)

While the hybridizer looks forward, the species fan looks backward...on the millennia to which we are the beneficiaries. Few are more enthusiastic and dedicated than these. Species is spoken in sub-groups of almost every society and species clubs are not uncommon. Inquire locally.

PERSPECTIVE.

There are limitations to ideal Phalaenopsis culture, some obvious, some not so obvious. Space limitation is one that affects most of us, all greenhouse or bench space being finite. That is true whether we have 3 or 3,000 square feet of bench space, but the solution to the problem is the same...bite the bullet peri-odically and purge the stuff that doesn't meet your current expectations or needs. Unless your livelihood depends on it, when you get one, get rid of one.

Most orchid growers have heard the old-timer's advice for greenhouse construction: "Figure what you need, then double it". I'd like to modify that; when you're done doubling it, cut it in half again, because that probably is all you can handle, *properly,* given the usual con-straints of earning a living and keeping up your Happy Home insurance. For every phal grow-er who underestimates his capacity to handle a given number of plants, there are at least 10 who go the other way and overestimate their ability to care for x-number of plants.

Be honest about it. We are a materialistic people and most orchid growers don't suffer too severely an incapacity to pay for more than they can tend to. (There is an uncomfort-able parallel with food here.) I won't lay the one on you that you can't be too rich or too thin, but the message should be clear.

In the purest sense, you can derive as much enjoyment from one plant in bloom at a time as you can from a thousand. Look at the serenity of Zen contemplation of simple things.

And you know what they call the urge to have more than you really need! Greed is a nasty word to be used in a book on orchids, but...

149

Time is another stricture and much of what I suggested above applies here as well. If time is a problem, avoid very small pots and slab mountings which require frequent waterings. Ditto on high-hung plants. Eliminate these types from your collection until you have more time to devote to them.

Pot a size larger than normal and you may be able to extend watering intervals to 7 days in the summer and 10 to 14 days in the winter. Automated, overhead watering is okay, but it is tricky in the short-day season and should be shut off during that time. Get a friend to come in and do your plants if you must be away...or board them at a nursery. It's a lot safer that way.

Unless you are a big-time grower or have trouble getting into the greenhouse on a regular basis to do your chores, don't waste your time trying to use an injector system to feed while you're away if you're not gone more than a week or two at a time...or even a month. The phals will do fine for that long without fertilizer (but not without water!), but water the day before feeding them.

The controller on an auto-watering system can be set to intervals up to 7 days and watering time can be varied for each individual 'zone' or group of plants.

One of the nice things about being a specialist is finding another soul who likes the same thing. Correspondence with these culture-kin can be the source of a great satisfaction. Every now and again I meet one of these friends I didn't know I had and get a shot of enthusiasm (and an infusion of new ideas) from the experience.

Whatever you decide to grow, do it with com- mitment and enthusiasm. The experience will brighten and lengthen your life. Come on in, the water's fine.

Section 18. PHALAENOPSIS AS CUT FLOWERS.

Sad to report, many floral designers avoid the use of cut Phalaenopsis blooms in flower arrangements and corsages, not because they don't like them, but because they don't know how to use them. There are several reasons for this.

The first of these is that to most arrangers, familiar with the stout ovary section of the Cattleya bloom, the slender, fragile-looking Phalaenopsis ovary section is a fright because the Cattleya can be pierced with wire to stiffen and bind their whole production together firmly. Do that with a phal and it probably will break off.

The trick in using phals in corsages or arrangements is to make a hairpin-shaped wire, wrapped in the center of its span with floratape, and slip it over the narrow base of the lip from the front with the open end of the hairpin pointed to the back. See photo.

Insert the hairpin all the way until the wrapped section touches the lip of the flower, pressing the two wires against the sides of the stem and wrap with floratape. Some arrangers route the wire *over* the column, some under. No matter, dealer's choice. With this stiffener, you may now proceed as with any other flower. As an added stiffener, some arrangers pierce the flower stem from one side to the other with a piece of wire and bend it back to align with the two ends of the hairpin and the flower stem.

A more common reason why cut phals aren't more popular with arrangers is because they usually collapse within 12 hours or so of the

time the corsage or arrangement was made. The result is an unsatisfied customer and a vow not to do *that* again. The answer to this problem is to

ALLOW CUT PHALAENOPSIS BLOOMS TO SOAK UP WATER FOR 3 HOURS AT ROOM TEMPERATURE BEFORE USING THEM.

Cut the blooms and allow them to stand in water for at least that long...it won't hurt in the least to make that 6 hours. Phals will stand in water at room temperature for 2 to 3 weeks or more. When you put the blooms in the water, note the ones that soak up the most water in the 3 hours. These are the ones which would have collapsed soon after being made up if not soaked this way.

Collapsed blooms can sometimes be revived by immersing them in ice water...tuck that one away for a future emergency.

AFTER THE FLOWER IS PUT INTO AN ARRANGEMENT, AND ONLY THEN, PUT THE WHOLE THING IN THE COOLER as usual to preserve it.

Do not chill before making up the arrangement or corsage. Cold flower stems are more brittle than warm ones and *will snap off.* Cooling phal blooms before use is the most common mistake in their use. It works with other orchids, but not phals.

The flat configuration of the Phalaenopsis bloom lends itself well to use in corsages because very little of the flower projects from the backing and offers little to catch milady's garments and virtually never touches (and tickles) her face the way cattleyas in corsages often do.

Many flower shop customers don't want to have phals used in their arrangements, because "It doesn't *look* like an orchid". Suggest the designer tell customers that it *is* an orchid, but a DIFFERENT one. No matter that the Phalaenopsis may be thousands of years old, if it is new on the market, it will have an attraction for a sizeable chunk of the buying public that is the trend-setting group. A Polaroid picture or two of some arrangements made with phals will help ease the customers into something unfamiliar.

Phal blooms are particularly well-suited as hair decorations. One or two in a flat hair piece looks lovely worn at the side or the back of the head and leaves the wearer completely free of the encumbrance a corsage often becomes.

An endearing quality of the Phalaenopsis to floral arrangers is their availability during the months of June and July when white cattleyas are very hard to come by. That probably will change with the development of a line of dependable, summer-blooming white catts, but in the meantime, plenty of white phals (summer spikes) are available for June weddings *if* the arrangers can be encouraged to use them. Worth remembering is that a cascading Phalaenopsis bridal bouquet is the picture of nuptial elegance.

A BIG ADVANTAGE PHALS HOLD OVER CATTLEYAS, AS THE STANDARD ORCHID, IS THE RANGE OF SIZES AVAILABLE.

The only really useful Cattleya size for corsages is the cocktail size or Japhet as it is known to arrangers (C. Henrietta Japhet is the standard), in the range of 3 to 4 inches in diameter. The more commonly available cabbages in the 5- to 7-inch size are just too big for the discriminating wearer, and there is almost nothing available in catts for the petite wearer who wants nothing larger than a 2-inch flower. Phalaenopsis has it all from 1 to 5 inches. The 2-inch size is just right for a man's boutonniere, too.

AND PHALS CAN BE DRAMATIC.

A very talented floral designer friend, Bob Bishop, recently 'did' a black tie fund raiser, in black and white. He made individual table pieces shown in the accompanying photos. The white Phalaenopsis blooms and candles stood out strikingly from the black silk ribbon, the dark greenery, the glass chimney and the mirror base. The original pieces were dusted with glitter to pick up highlights and add a touch of finesse and enchantment. Black and white is a color combination avoided by many floral designers, but, as you can see, there is much to recommend it with white Phalaenopsis blooms as the featured attraction.

If you cut phal spikes for use in arrangements, be sure to leave at least one or two nodes on the bottom of the spike to bloom again in 45 to 60 days.

Hugo Freed advises that the big whites open a new flower on a spike every 3 to 5 days after the first one and a large, strong plant can easily produce 30 to 40 flowers on 3 spikings in a season without overtaxing the plant. The key to a long flowering season for cut flowers is to chill the plants at night starting about August the 1st and cutting spikes off completely by mid-May to force the plant to rest. (*This* schedule, of course, instead of the normal nighttime chilling beginning in October; cut-flower growers take note.)

152

Phalaenopsis bloom with hairpin

Hairpin inserted (left) and rear view (right)

'Elegance in black and white'
By Bob Bishop

CHAPTER FOUR

A GOOD PLACE TO GROW PHALAENOPSIS

Section 19. GREENHOUSE STUFF ...MODIFICATIONS AND IDEAS.

The place you have in which to grow your phals, be it a windowsill, a glass case, a light cart, a lath house, or greenhouse, needs certain features. These include a means of varying the amount of light reaching the plants; a means of maintaining temperatures between 62 and 85°F; a means of moving large quantities of air about; a means of maintaining a minimum relative humidity of 50% and; a means of supporting the plants in the stream of moving air.

How you provide these amenities to the plants can be categorized as good, better or best. I've outlined previously what is needed; now I'm going to suggest how to do it and maybe how to do it better or even best.

Section 19.1 LIGHT CONTROL.

On a windowsill, a lace curtain or a sheer does a pretty good job of reducing light reaching your plants, but the amount of shading must be changed from time to time to keep up with seasonal changes in sunlight angle and intensity. A tree, whose leaves were 'dappling' your phal's light in the summer can lose those leaves in October when the sun's rays are still strong enough to sunburn the plant. Ditto for greenhouses. Laths or shade cloth can be used on a greenhouse or lath house to reduce light, too, but they have to be removed in winter to maintain the needed amount of light.

The most convenient, safest and cheapest method of light control on a glass or plastic roof or sidewalls is shading compound.

It will not, however, do much for the structure's appearance, but then again, neither will shade cloth. Looks like hell is what it does.

Shading compound is available at most nursery supply houses at only small cost. It used to be called whitewash when I was a kid; same stuff. The canned stuff is more expensive. Use the material that comes in 25-pound bags...you'll have a continuing need for it.

Shading compound can be applied with a hand-operated garden pump sprayer **IF DILUTED TO ONE-QUARTER THE RECOMMENDED CONSISTENCY.** Start thin and add layers or coats until your light levels are where you want them. If rain is a frequent occurrence in your locality, add a teaspoon of white latex paint to a gallon of mix before spraying it on. Don't use more than this unless you live in a rain forest or you'll wind up scrubbing paint off your glass when you want more light...I know.

In the dryer climates, use no paint binder and spray the shade compound solution lightly after a few showers to renew the coating. It lasts quite a while with no paint additives. Hose it off to increase light in the house in stages. Spray a little detergent and water on first if it persists, and brush if it is really stuck on.

Fiberglass greenhouse roofing crazes after a few years in the hot sun and will not give up its coating of shading compound easily, but that should not be a problem. If it is, either replace the plastic with Filon or its equivalent, or scrub the surface with water and steel wool and then put on a coat of clear brushing lacquer. That should last another few years.

If you have high shelves or grow plants up near the glass, put the coating of shade compound on a little bit thicker over them. If your greenhouse has semi-transparent sidewalls, spray those, too. Lower sun angles in autumn can sunburn plants near the glass. Wet surrounding structures and shrubs with a hose before spraying on the shade compound. That will make it easier to hose off the unwanted overspray which is inevitable.

The idea is to spray a light coating of the shade compound on the roof, wait a little for it to dry, then go inside and read the light with your newly-purchased light meter. If it's OK, leave it. If it's too much, add a bit more shade. If you have too much shade, wash a little off. Piece of cake. Precise light control. No more excuses for mediocre flowers. Better blooms. Wow 'em at club meetings.

Use of the inexpensive corrugated plastic roofing for your greenhouse is false economy. The inexpensive stuff will last 2 years at best, less in sun-intensive areas, before it begins to block out too much light. You won't notice it, but your plants will.

Filon or its equivalent is best...use the 4-ounce (per square foot) stuff unless wind or snow loads are a problem in your area. Use the 5-ounce if they are. It costs more, of course.

Regarding building permits to build a greenhouse...be advised that many building inspectors who have little experience with greenhouses think they should be built like a house, in some cases like a block house.

There are all kinds of horror stories floating around about the dumb things they've made people do before they'd pass a greenhouse. A friend of mine had one inspector demand he

put in a 4x12-inch ridgepole in his new greenhouse. Only a 1x8 is used in home construction! He had to put in so much overhead bracing to satisfy the guy that now his plants don't get enough light. If we ever have 300 mph winds or 14 feet of snow in southern California, Richard Swift is ready. He's got the only overhead lumber yard around. Anyway, do what your conscience demands.

Section 19.2 TEMPERATURE CONTROL.

Gas heat in cold weather is cheapest (relatively) and an evaporative cooler in the warm, dry weather works well if you require cooling in your location. Evaporative coolers, long used in the dry southwest, provide both cooling and humidity. The dryer the outside air, the better the cooler works.

If you don't need cooling in the warm weather, make sure you have ample vent capacity for fresh air and possibly a powered vent. Remember to provide an *inlet* for the cool air as well as an *outlet* for the warm. Locating the inlets low and outlets high will give you the most efficient air exchange process. Locate your high, outlet vent away from the direction of the prevailing winds. Ridge vents are most efficient. If the prevailing winds are from the west, say, in the warm weather, locate your warm air outlet on the east side of the greenhouse so the low pressure resulting from structure wind-shadow can be used to remove stale and possibly hot air from the greenhouse.

Thermostatic control for heat and cooling is far and away the most convenient, most accurate, and, in terms of safety, is the cheapest. Use a 'millivolt' thermostat if you can and match it with a 'millivolt' gas valve on the gas heater. The voltage used to operate the gas valve of the heater is generated by a thermo-couple in the pilot light flame. If you have an electrical power outage in cold weather with this kind of apparatus, the heater will continue to work; the blower won't, but at least you have *some* heat and it may be enough to save your plants in severely cold weather during a power outage.

If you have the standard 12-or 24-volt system of heater control in the same circumstances, you can start saying your Hail Marys. I know of many orchid growers in the desert south-west of the US, without a dime's worth of pro-tection in case of a power outage or other malfunction of heating/cooling equipment... and this with thousands of dollars worth of orchid plants inside. Growers in the warm cli-mates are especially vulnerable to this kind of weather-caused disaster. It isn't a question of *whether* weather extremes will happen, only *when*. Within a week of this writing televi-sion newscasts have carried stories of 24°F. temperatures in Miami, Florida and 105 mile per hour winds in the South of England. It happens...and

YOU COULD LOSE YOUR ENTIRE COL-LECTION IN A MATTER OF HOURS.

It happens over and over. Ask Gary Stanley of Winnipeg or Len Ellentuch of Wallkill, NY. Everything lost. And there are others.

Do I have your attention? Good. Effective solutions are available at very nominal cost. *Read How to Cope With a Power Outage* in the next section for some of them.

Heat provided *under* the plants seems to be of greater benefit than heat provided around the plants. Seedlings grow much more quickly when given bottom heat with either finned or tube-heat conduits. Use of plastic film tubes to distribute warm air in a greenhouse is popu-lar and highly recommended.

If you're using a windowsill or enclosed porch or the like to grow phals, bring them into the warmest part of the house on cold nights. A small electrical heater can keep the chill off the plants in a small, enclosed space. A plastic tent over the plants and heater will help, but keep the plastic safely away from the heating element. Try to get a heater with a thermostat.

In the house, check the minimum temperature on your thermostat. Some of the newer ones allow minimum temps down to the low 50's. The older ones have a baseline temperature of 59 to 60 degrees F.

A HIGH-LOW THERMOMETER IS VERY USEFUL WITH ANY NEW ARRANGE-MENT FOR TEMPERATURE CONTROL.

It records the minimum and maximum tem-peratures it has been exposed to and holds an indication of those readings for your reading. Good in the greenhouse, too...no, not good, essential.

A light bulb, particularly an infrared heating lamp, will do in a pinch to keep your phals warm. But watch it closely for a while before leaving your pretties in its hands. Remember, too, that anything shaded from its radiation *will not be heated.*

Section 19.3 AIR MOVEMENT.

With only a few plants, not to worry; but with more than just a few, you'll need moving air, so provide a fan that can run from now on. Horizontal fans will do, but overhead ceiling fans are best, particularly if they blow *upward*, getting a boost from rising currents of warm air in your greenhouse. Run it just fast enough to move cigarette smoke in the corners of the growing area (not necessarily under the benches) at night and enough to move smoke smartly by day. Slow at night, fast at day...or fast all the time. It uses less power when slowed at night, if that is a consideration.

The reason for faster running during the day is to disperse heat from solar radiation. With horizontal fans, try to set up a circulation of air along one side of the house and the fan will draw air back along the other side. Pointed low in the center of your growing space is not so good. Try the other ways.

Section 19.4 HUMIDITY CONTROL

Where humidity in your home is not sufficient for the phals, a tray of wet gravel is quite a satisfactory solution. For a greenhouse, a misting system is easy to install and solves virtually all your low humidity problems. There's a diagram in this section for an easily-assembled one if you are reasonably at home with things electrical.

The components for this system are a 24-volt transformer, a 24-volt lawn sprinkler solenoid shutoff valve, a humidistat, an on-off test switch, misting heads and connecting wires and plumbing. Most parts are available in hardware stores except the misting heads or nozzles (use the 1 gallon per minute size). They can be gotten from local greenhouse suppliers or California Greenhouse Controls, 3266 North Rosemead Blvd., El Monte, CA 91731. Geiger in Harleyville, PA also has them.

The floor of the greenhouse should be covered with 1 to 2 inches of pea-sized gravel which will serve as an evaporative medium when wet.

Use one misting head for each 50 to 75 square feet of greenhouse floor space. Run the supply tubing or plastic pipe along the foundation with the nozzles pointing in toward the center of the greenhouse at a slight angle above the level. The idea is to make the largest possible spray pattern on the gravel for maximum evaporation. A perfect spray pattern would be one in which every bit of the gravel on the greenhouse floor would be wet by the misting nozzles.

If you have sand in your water supply (not unusual) clean out the screens in the misting heads periodically.

Mount the humidity controller at about eye-level along with the thermostat and other environmental control units. You will find the 'OFF' and 'TEST' positions on the misting system control handy, but a simple on-off switch will do or you can start and stop the system by raising and lowering the humidity control setting. This is a handy accessory when you want to walk through the greenhouse and the misting system is going. Better than wet feet.

The overhead fan will do a good job of moving the humidity from ground level up to where the plants are.

A variation on this system integrating a power-off emergency heating and cooling system is covered in Section 20, next.

Section 19.5 PLANT SUPPORT.

Plant support or benches can take many different forms, but there are some basic needs. First, the benches should be at a level convenient for you, be it knee-high, waist-high or any point in between.

If you have a choice in the matter, make the top of the bench at a level even with the tips of your thumbs as you stand relaxed in front of it. Go lower and you'll strain your back reaching for plants at the back of the bench; go higher and you won't be able to reach them.

Make the bench no deeper from front to back than you can reach comfortably; 36 inches for most men, 30 inches for most of the ladies.

TOO WIDE A BENCH WILL MAKE YOU JUST A LITTLE RETICENT ABOUT PICKING UP A PLANT FOR INSPECTION AT THE BACK; AND THAT CAN BECOME A HABIT...OF NEGLECT.

It should go without saying that the bench should have enough support to hold a mass of heavy, wet plants. You will see sagging wire bench tops in many greenhouses...with pots tipping every which way, including over.

Circulating air in the greenhouse must be free to pass between and around the plants. Laths or 1 x 2's handle the support function well enough, but come up a little short on allowing air to circulate through the bench. They also provide dandy places for slugs and snails to spend their sleeping hours in the daytime.

Wire fabric is an ideal medium for plant support and for air circulation. The 1" x 2" welded fabric is a good choice and is available in 100-foot rolls as well as shorter lengths. The wire fabric can be bent to shape to make step benches or flat benches with a bent-up lip to hold plants at the edge in place.

THERE IS A GREAT DEAL TO BE SAID IN FAVOR OF A WELDED-WIRE FABRIC STEP BENCH FOR PHALAENOPSIS CULTURE.

For a start, you can grow 30 to 40% *more* plants on a step bench than on a flat bench of equal (floor) space. Large phal leaves can droop without touching the pot on the next lower step. See photo. If you spread the leaves of mature phals like that on a flat bench, you'd have room for fewer than half as many plants as on a comparable-sized step bench. More leaf area of any given plant will see more direct sunlight on a step and, as a consequence, the plant will synthesize more food and grow more and faster.

Curiously, after a few years on a south-facing step bench, many Phalaenopsis plants will have all their leaves grouped in a 120 degrees-or-so arc facing the sun. Flowers, of course, bloom, for the most part facing the same direction. Everything the plant has to offer is focused in that 120 degrees. The net effect of massed, flowering, mature phals, in the spring, on a step bench...is stunning.

Light-colored flowers contrast dramatically with the green leaf background. I have the north side of my phal house covered with plywood, so no light enters from that direction at all, making the forward focus of the plants even more emphatic.

Another use for a south-facing wire step bench (north-facing for Aussies and Afrikaners) is as a finishing bench for plants you intend to show for awards. Put them in place as soon as possible after the spikes emerge...and leave them undisturbed until they flower.

Air circulation with welded wire fabric is probably the best that can be had in plant culture, especially if an up-draft ceiling fan is used. (see figure on greenhouse air circulation). It's also easy to tilt each plant a little toward the light to improve its view of the sun, and more importantly, to drain the crowns quicker. Fewer rot problems. The lowest step on the step bench is for low-light rest for recuperating plants and a place for plants in spike to fatten their buds.

NORTH-FACING STEP BENCHES HAVE NO USE IN THE NORTHERN HEMI-SPHERE... EXCEPT AS AN EXAMPLE OF DUMB THINGS NO ONE SHOULD DO. DITTO SOUTH-FACING STEP BENCHES IN THE SOUTHERN HEMISPHERE.

The welded-wire fabric comes in 3- and 4-foot widths and can be bent over a bench edge to a 90 degree angle. A 9-foot length (actually 9'2" to allow for the top shelf's back lip) can be bent to yield a vertical section 6-feet high and with six 6-inch shelves, each with a vertical height of 12 inches.

The angled 74-inch 2 x 4's should be spaced the width of your wire fabric. (For a more permanent arrangement, use galvanized tubing which is intended as top rail for chain link fences.) To attach the bent wire section; level, align and tack the wire in place with a staple gun where it touches the angled support. With galvanized tubing, drill and drive heavy sheet metal screws almost all the way in. Rest the wire on the screw and tighten.

Follow up later with hog-wire staples...or use a staple gun that shoots U-shaped staples (for use in securing electrical cable) in the first place.

Water deionizing system tanks.
Water passes through the acid tank on the left, through the hydroxide tank on the right and out into the system.

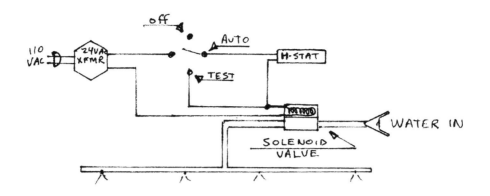

Misting System Schematic Diagram

Why large phal plants are happy on stepped benches.

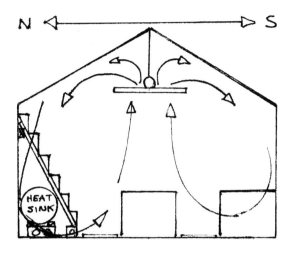

Greenhouse air circulation

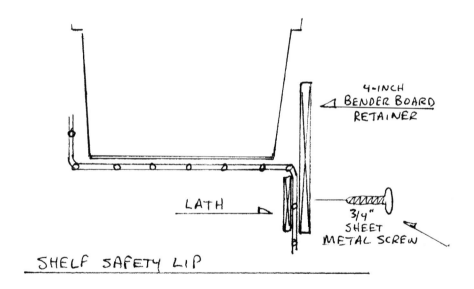

Step bench safety lip.

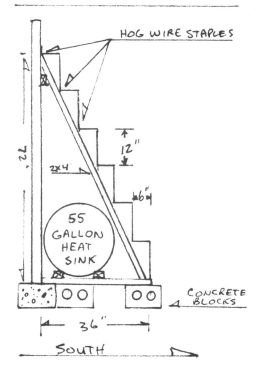

WIRE STEP BENCH
6" SHELVES - 12" RISE

HOG WIRE STAPLES

12"

2X4

6"

55 GALLON HEAT SINK

CONCRETE BLOCKS

36"

SOUTH

Step bench schematic

Step bench detail.

164

Welded wire step bench facing south.

The top shelf is a bit of a stretch for me and I'm six-one. If that's too much of a reach, make only 5 shelves for a total of 5 feet high and 30 inches out from the wall. Or make it as described and leave the top shelf vacant. That's not too bad an idea, because it improves the air flow down from the fan and under the step bench. That top row is quite close to the glass, anyway, and needs more frequent watering than the rest.

FACE THE STEP BENCH TO THE SOUTH OR YOU WILL LOSE MANY OF ITS BENEFITS.

There's room under a 15-foot long section of 6-foot high step bench for four 55-gallon drums of water that serve as over three-quarters of a ton of heat sink and energy savings. More on this in Section 20. (If you decide to put drums under the step bench for use as a heat sink, put them in place *before* attaching the bent-wire forms. Otherwise, it's hernia city. I know. Also, do I need to add that you put the water in the drums *after* you put them in place? Nah!)

I've added a safety edge to each shelf in the form of a 4-inch wide redwood 'bender board', commonly used to edge gardens. I added it to keep the top heavy mature plants from toppling over...in an earthquake. (This *is* California, the land of the movers and shakers) It also serves to keep large plants upright when flowers get wet and want to fall over.

A handy use for any left over welded wire fabric is as a grid for hanging plants from the greenhouse ceiling. Suspend or attach a piece of 1/2-inch electrical metallic tubing (EMT) in an open area of your greenhouse. Lace a 6-inch wide strip of the welded wire fabric to a length of EMT with wire. It's best to run the EMT north to south, but east to west is almost as good.

Punch holes in the plant pot rims about an inch below the top. An adjustable hole-puncher works just fine. Fashion an S-hook from coat hanger-sized galvanized wire and crimp it in place in the hole. Stripped, number 12 electrical cable works well, too. Hang it in the top row of openings of the grid and hang plants on *both* sides for balance and best use of the space. (Remember to use a finer grade of potting medium in these high-hung plants. Seedling mix will do just fine. They are going to dry out faster than those on the benches below.)

Section 20. ENERGY-SAVING IDEAS.

Greenhouses are horrendously wasteful of heating and cooling energy and a few improvements, even minor ones, can bring about a dramatic savings to your utility bills.

The UC Cooperative Extension, recently did a study which concluded that

68% OF HEAT LOSS IN GREENHOUSES WENT OUT THROUGH THE ROOF.

It follows, then, that double- or triple-glazing your greenhouse roof will do more to reduce your heating and cooling bills than almost any other single improvement you could make.

THE RETURN YOU WILL GET ON DOUBLE-GLAZING A GREENHOUSE ROOF FOR INSULATION IS GOING TO PAY FOR ITSELF IN VERY SHORT ORDER, PROBABLY IN THE FIRST HEATING/ COOLING SEASON. START YOUR GREENHOUSE IMPROVEMENT PROGRAM THERE.

An inner lining of the greenhouse roof, for example, will save 40 to 50% of the energy loss there, and that loss represents 68% of the total loss for the whole house. Bottom line: double line the roof of your greenhouse and save between 27 and 34% of your heating bill! If you are spending $100 now, (don't you wish) it will cost you between $66 and $73 after lining your greenhouse roof with film plastic. (UC,1982)

I've had excellent results with a three-layer plastic material called Griffolyn, made by Reef Industries, P.O. Box 750250, Houston,

Texas, USA 77275-9988. It has two layers of plastic sheet with a nylon mesh in between to give the material dimensional stability and keep it from sagging over the years.

Used under a plastic roofing material that has an ultra-violet filter built in...and most of the good stuff today does...it will last a long time. Even here on the desert it lasts at least 8 years. Highly recommended.

On a redwood and glass greenhouse, I added a Filon fiberglass, corrugated outer glazing with about one and one-half inches of dead air space between the plastic and the glass. To that I added a glazing of Griffolyn on the *inside* of the house, triple-glazing the roof.

Installation of an inner envelope in a greenhouse is a labor-intensive task, that is, the cost of the labor of putting it in place is a major cost factor when compared with the cost of materials...so long life was high on my list of priorities for a liner. With the entrained nylon mesh, Griffolyn sags very little. That's important not only for cosmetic purposes, but also because the insulation value of the dead air space decreases as the separation increases over 4 inches...just about the thickness of the rafters, so no sagging, please.

After 8 years in place and exposed to very high solar radiation, as you can see from the photo, it is still tight as a drum.

Third, and perhaps most important, is Griffolyn's customer service program. They have a toll free number (1-800-231-6074) to call in Houston, TX and I called with a technical question. The sales manager took the call and answered my question and then some. I like that.

I'm impressed with the product and the company. If I had Victor Kiam's money, (he's the president of Remington Products and a television commercial personality) I'd buy the company.

The commonly available PVC is not satisfactory for our purpose because it will not last a single season in our fierce, southwestern US summers...and not much longer elsewhere.

Another reason for using an innerlining is that it not only provides insulation, but also serves to reduce air leaks or infiltration that makes up another 21% of greenhouse heat loss in the winter, reason enough alone to put one in.

BESIDES, AFTER YOU'VE BEEN IN AN UNINSULATED GREENHOUSE, AN INSULATED ONE JUST *FEELS* SNUGGER AND MORE COMFORTABLE. It's like the difference between an empty room and one with a carpet on the floor.

For those of you who have suffered with dripping condensation on your plants throughout the heating season, an inner lining for your greenhouse is like having an umbrella in a rainstorm.

Oddly enough, with dead air spaces, you can have too much of a good thing. Insulation value of a dead air space increases as the thickness of the air space increases from zero to 3/4ths of an inch; it remains constant up to about 4 inches and decreases from 4 inches on up. Convection currents begin to operate at that point, decreasing the insulation value. (Langdon,1980) Read: 3/4ths of an inch of air gap is enough to get maximum insulation value.

I set the corrugated plastic off the glass roof by using 1 x 2 inch furring strips attached with screws to the redwood glazing bars. Drywall screws work beautifully with a power screwdriver. Get the galvanized type.

Why not use nails? Think about it.

The fiberglass is also screwed to the 1 x 2's, and the screws sealed with silicone caulking on the sides and top, but not the bottom. Drainage.

Sidewalls of the greenhouse are double-glazed...with fiberglass and Griffolyn only. Losses from sides constitute only 10% of the total losses. On the north side, no glazing is necessary since only a trace of skylight enters from that direction. I used 3/8ths-inch exterior plywood, painted white on the inside to reflect direct light back to the plants, and a film plastic inner sheath for insulation and to stop air infiltration.

The plywood will help reduce heat losses from cold north winds in the winter. Run the film plastic on all four walls on the inside all the way down to the foundation to insulate and to stop drafts.

Our American pioneer forefathers managed to extend the vegetable growing season in cold climates by digging large holes that are now called cold frames or sunpits...and glazing over the top. Earth heat supplemented by solar radiation kept temperatures high enough to sustain the crop. We can use the principle by burying a greenhouse to bench level in the ground...a semi-sunpit. If possible, 2-inch styrofoam insulation should be put down before the floor is poured and also applied to the sidewalls before backfill is done to prevent heat loss.

A semi-sunpit greenhouse with styrofoam insulation and double- or triple-glazing would be appreciably less costly to operate than an above ground, uninsulated greenhouse would. Amortization of the improvements would vary with refinements and local energy costs, but could well be in the 4- to 6-year range in the Middle West of the US.

A simple, but effective, way to dampen the swings of daytime high temperatures and nighttime lows is through a passive measure called heat sinks. A heat sink is any material that absorbs heat when the ambient temperature is higher than its internal temperature...and gives it up when the reverse is true. A heat sink can be a stone wall, a tile floor, a container of water...or anything that is a good conductor of heat, but we are interested in those that are efficient and cheap. Water is by far the best choice by reason of cost, efficiency and availability.(Mazria,1979)

I put four 50-gallon drums of water under the step bench mentioned earlier for this purpose. I found that water temperatures in the drums differed, on an average winter day, by 5° F. between day-end highs and night-end lows. A BTU is the amount of heat required to raise one pound of water one degree F. at or near 40 degrees. Multiply 1600 pounds of water by 5 degrees and you have about 8,000 BTUs, minus some losses, **AT ABSOLUTELY NO RECURRING COST.**

When I found that, I looked around for other cheap ways to hold water in the greenhouses. What I found was empty gallon wine jugs...lots of them. Even when the wine is gone, they go on serving mankind. I get misty-eyed just thinking about them.

Concrete walkways are heat sinks, too. And they are a lot easier on the feet than gravel or duck boards.

I have a friend in Phoenix who had a hot tub in his greenhouse. What it is is a 500-gallon heat sink that can be used for social purposes. Neat. I wish I had room.

The back-to-earthers recommend a sizeable fishtank in the greenhouse as a passive heat sink.

A tank of water in the greenhouse could serve several purposes: (1) a holding point in the winter until cold tap water mellows enough to be used on the plants; (2) a holding point while harmful additives to your drinking water dissipate; and (3) a reservoir for holding heat collected in an *active* solar heat collection system with collectors and a pump. These in addition to serving as a passive heat sink. If the tank is a spa, it becomes a social center as well.

A greenhouse is, of course, a solar collector. If you have an attached or lean-to greenhouse, you probably already know you can use it to heat your house, at least partially, in the winter...and live among your orchids.

A couple of inexpensive, energy-saving improvements that can also protect your beauties in the event of a power outage or heater/cooler malfunction are outlined in an article I did that appeared in the January 1982 issue of the American Orchid Society *Bulletin*. If you are concerned about the ability of your orchids to survive in a power outage, read the piece.

Griffolyn insulation inner-lining.

California heat sink.

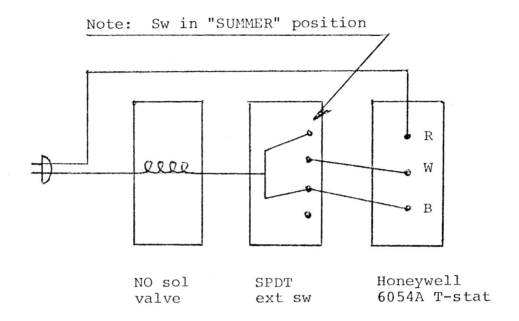

Note: Sw in "SUMMER" position

NO sol   SPDT   Honeywell
valve   ext sw   6054A T-stat

Wiring diagram
Emergency heating and cooling system.

Space-saving suspension system
for high-hung plants.

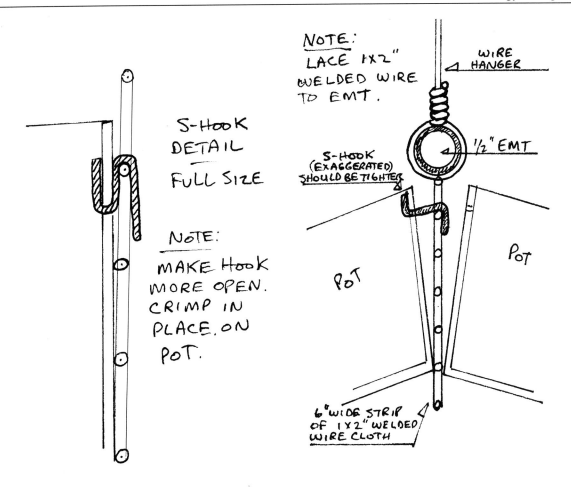

S-HOOK
DETAIL

FULL SIZE

NOTE:
MAKE HOOK
MORE OPEN.
CRIMP IN
PLACE. ON
POT.

NOTE:
LACE 1×2"
WELDED WIRE
TO EMT.

WIRE
HANGER

S-HOOK
(EXAGGERATED)
SHOULD BE TIGHTER

½" EMT

POT

POT

6" WIDE STRIP
OF 1×2" WELDED
WIRE CLOTH

Hanger details...high storage.

Section 20.1

HOW TO COPE WITH A POWER OUTAGE
(Energy-Saving Greenhouse Insurance.)

Most of us who rely on electrically-operated equipment to protect our plants in the heat of the summer and the cold of the winter live in dread of a power outage, especially in our absence. While the problem is more acute here, it also exists elsewhere in the temperate areas that include all of the continental US, Europe, South Africa and Australia.

Temperatures, even in a vented greenhouse, can quickly reach the point of irreversible damage in the summer months when the power goes off and the same is true in the winter. I've incorporated some features in my greenhouses to cope with the power-out spectre here on the edge of the desert where summertime temperatures frequently range from 105 to 115 degrees F., features you may be able to use in yours. As an added bonus, they save energy.

The basic package that complements shade cloth (or shade compound), an automatic misting system, and an evaporative cooler for summertime environmental control includes a heat motor-operated vent (non-electrical), a thermal chimney and an outside, overhead sprinkler system.

HEAT MOTOR VENT.

The heat motor is a temperature-sensitive device that uses expansion or contraction of a gas confined in a cylinder to open or close a vent port. Generally, the fixed-range heat motors begin to open at about 65 degrees F. and are fully open as the temperature rises to 75 degrees. The reverse is true as the temperature falls.

Now, most greenhouses have a screened inlet through which air can enter to provide a cooling flow through the greenhouse and out the open vent in warm weather. The function of the heat motor is to open and close the top vent as the temperatures rise and fall. In a power-out situation, convection currents may provide the only air movement in the house since fans and blowers are inoperative. It is only a small movement, of course, but it may be movement enough to save your beauties. Installation of this automatic vent is the first step in providing power-out insurance for your greenhouse.

SOLAR CHIMNEY.

Power-off air movement in the greenhouse can be improved through the use of a solar chimney attached to a greenhouse opening. The chimney is an 8-foot high box, a foot square, covered on three sides with clear fiberglass and plywood on the fourth. (A taller chimney will give a greater draw, but an 8-footer will do nicely.) A 7-foot length of 12-inch diameter stove pipe, painted flat black, runs up the center and is topped with an attic ventilating turbine, slightly modified.

Solar energy heats the pipe which, in turn, heats the air inside. The air rises, starting the chimney effect. The chimney effect is boosted by the already-heated air from the top reaches of the greenhouse which rises in a thermal current in the chimney.

The pick-off point for the chimney should be at the hottest point of the top inside of the greenhouse. (The opening to the chimney can be closed off during cold weather to prevent heat loss.) The chimney effect is further boosted by a slight low pressure condition which exists around the turbine when a breeze blows.

I added a blade from a discarded electric fan to the shaft of the turbine for a little more help. If you do the same, be sure the fan matches the direction of turbine rotation.

The net effect of all these boosts in a power-out situation is not a dramatic blast of hot air up the chimney, but rather, a steady, continuous flow which has the advantage of costing nothing to operate. The chimney effect is enough to draw a soul-satisfying stream of cool air in through the evaporative cooler, or any other opening, even when electrical power is on and the evaporative cooler, if you have one, is not running.

USED IN A GREENHOUSE WITHOUT A COOLER, THE SOLAR CHIMNEY WILL PROVIDE MOST, IF NOT ALL, THE VENTILATION REQUIRED DURING WARM WEATHER.

You can see that this process is going to draw off some heat accumulating early on a summer morning until the build-up catches up and turns on the cooler or vent fan. The net effect is a later starting and earlier stopping of the cooler. The system is a negative resistance vent which provides an acceptable temperature in the greenhouse when used with the overhead sprinkler system, even on a 105-degree day with no electrical power. With the cooler operating, it provides a low-resistance path for high, hot air to exit.

OVERHEAD SPRINKLER SYSTEM

The outside overhead sprinkler system uses the temperature of tap water as a greenhouse temperature control medium.

THE HEART OF THE SYSTEM IS A SOLENOID-OPERATED, 110 VAC WATER SHUTOFF VALVE WHICH IS CLOSED WHEN POWER IS ON.

When the power goes off, the valve opens sending water (at about 60-65 degrees F. locally year round) through a pipe to sprinklers on the greenhouse roof to cool the entire house until power comes back on...at which time the valve closes and the water stops. I have a roof manifold connected to the greenhouse misting system, through a check valve, to continue cooling inside in a power-out situation which would normally shut the misters off.

Although the sprinkler system could be installed inside the greenhouse, that might be messy and does not keep the heat outside as does the other method.

The sprinkler system operation can be improved by adding a thermostat in a control loop to turn the water on when greenhouse temperatures go too high or too low, even if power is still on. (I use a Honeywell Model 6054A, a heating and cooling thermostat.)

With the temperature setting at 90 degrees on the heating side, the thermostat will open above that temperature and remove the power from the shutoff valve, opening it and starting the cooling shower.

This is handy for the all too frequent situation that exists when a fan belt breaks in the evaporative cooler and cooling stops even though the power is still on.

Same problem with a vent fan going out in a greenhouse that relies on it for summertime cooling.

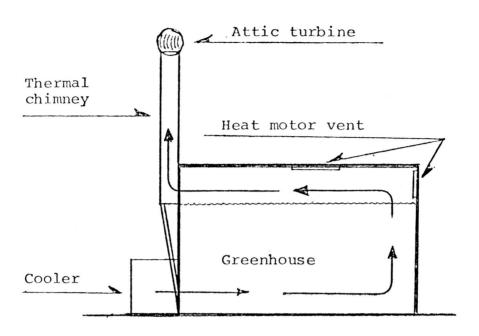

Greenhouse side elevation

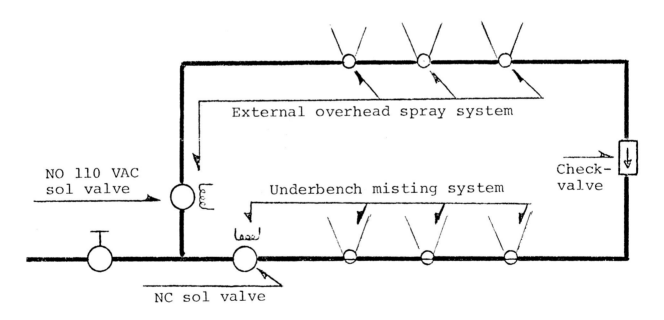

Plumbing system for emergency
cooling and heating system.

A very useful variation on this control was suggested by Dr. Bob Engel of the University of Redlands, wherein adding an external switch to the thermostat will provide a winter-summer selection of operation. In this way, the same 65-degree water can be pumped on to the outside of the greenhouse on very cold nights, when the power goes off, or when a heater goes off.

I keep a winter setting of 55 degrees on the cooling side of the thermostat in my greenhouses and when tested on a rare 32-degree night here, inside temperature stabilized at 47 degrees; not great, but enough to save the orchids.

My greenhouse is Filon plastic-covered and, when the admittedly unscientific tests were done, I had 55% shade cloth installed. I have since switched to shade compound and increased the shade for the phals and improved the summertime figures slightly from the power-off, stabilized, 87 degrees inside with an outside air temperature of 105 degrees F.

The solar chimney and heat-motor vent combine to shorten the running time of my evaporative cooler in the summer months. At this writing, in August, the cooler runs 7-8 hours per day in maintaining an 87 degree maximum. This is 3-4 hours less than before the changes were made, so in addition to protection from extremes in greenhouse temperatures, I have a tidy savings in my electric utility bill as well. The cooler comes on later, goes off earlier, and makes absolute control of maximum greenhouse temperatures a reality. (The additional shading undoubtedly helped.)

The normally-open water shutoff valve is available from California Greenhouse

Controls Company, 3266 N. Rosemead Blvd., El Monte, CA 91731, as is a variable setting heat-motor vent actuator. A less sophisticated, fixed temperature range model heat motor actuator is available from Dalen Products, Inc., 201 Sherlake Drive, Knoxville, TN 37922.

The solar chimney referred to above is simple to make. The plywood and plastic are nailed to 2 x 2's which extend the full height of the box. Plastic is used on the east, south and west sides down to the 'hip' where plywood is used on three sides. The fourth side is the opening into the greenhouse...which should have a cabinet door with a magnetic catch installed. I put a 3-foot long piece of heavy wire on the door to open and close it from below.

The 'feet', which stand on the greenhouse supporting members, are 2 x 4's. Lag bolts and machine bolts and nuts secure the chimney to the greenhouse. Guy wires attached to the top of the chimney, through the 2 x 2's and the chimney pipe, stabilize the structure in winds which around here reach 70 mph during the winter. The chimney pipe is hung inside the whole box and rests on the inside of the 'hips'. It is secured at the top. Not very pretty, but functional as hell.

IN CLOSING THIS BOOK:

I guess there really is no closing to this book or to the subject, either, because at this point probably the best thing you could do is to lay it down and pick it up again when things are not going the way they should...then re-read a section when you need help. We don't read and learn things all at once, then throw our books away...because our receptivity to new learning depends in large measure on how much we already know. It's amazing how much more you can get from a text when you are another year into a subject. Even if you don't think you need help, re-read it, OK? Does that make any sense?

For what it's worth and with no explanation, I re-learn more on the subject every time I go back over this text. I think that must have something to do with age, but I'm not going to ask. I've heard there are three signs of aging; one is a loss of memory and...I've forgotten the other two.

But, re-reading the book can't be such a bad idea. Use it for reference the rest of the time.

Now, if I don't go and clean the garage, my happy home insurance is going to expire. Nancy says if I don't get on it, there won't be any more books. So I'd better.

Good luck with your phals.

> Bob Gordon
> Rialto, California
> May 1990

CHAPTER FIVE

ALSO

Section 21. SOME SOURCES OF PHALAENOPSIS PLANTS AND SUPPLIES

ABC Orchids
3154 N.E. Evangeline Thwy
Lafayette, LA 70507

Botany Bay Orchids
P.O. Box 811
Bowral, NSW 2576 AUSTRALIA

Butterfly Orchids
821 W. Ballina Ct
Newbury Park, CA 91320

Carmela Orchids
P.O. Box H
Hakalau, HI 96710

Coqui Nurseries
P.O. Box M
Bayamon, PR 00620

DeRosa Orchids
212 W. Central St
Natick, MA 01760

East Hill Orchids
325 Piermont Rd
Closter, NJ 07624

John Ewing Orchids
P.O. Box 1318
Soquel, CA 95073

Frier's Orchids
P.O. Box 8772
Woodcliff Lake, NJ 07675

Greenaway Orchids
Rookery Farm, Puxton nr
Weston SM, Avon BS24 6TL UK

H & R Nurseries
41-240 Hihimanu St
Waimanalo, HI 96795

Humpybong Orchid Nursery
38 Collins St
Woody Point, QLD 4019 AUSTRALIA

J & M Tropicals
9527 Pinecone Dr
Cantonment, FL 32533

Jungle Gems
300 Edgewood Rd
Edgewood, MD 21040

Kodama Orchid Nursery
86-379 Lualualei Hmstd Rd
Waianae, HI 96792

Krull-Smith Orchids
Ponkan Rd, Rt 3, Box 18a
Apopka, FL 32703

Leilehua Orchids
166 Kaliko Dr
Wahiawa, HI 96786

Rod McLellan Co
1450 El Camino Real
South San Francisco, CA 94080

Miller's Orchids
2021 Margie Lane
Anaheim, CA 92802

Norman's Orchid Nursery
11039 Monte Vista Ave
Ontario, CA 91761

Oak Hill Gardens
P.O. Box 25, Rt 2, Binnie Rd
Dundee, IL 60118

Orchid Carousel
10116 Independence Ave
Chatsworth, CA 91311

Orchid Plantation
400 N. Fig Tree Lane
Plantation, FL 33317

Orchid World Intl
11295 S.W. 93rd St
Miami, FL 33176

Orchids by Hausermann
2N 134 Addison Rd
Villa Park, IL 60181

Orchids by Mellott
521 Wenzell Ave
Pittsburgh, PA 15216

Orchids by Vicli
3738 Ditzler
Kansas City, KS 64133

The Phally House
33 Hinekura Ave
Taupo, NEW ZEALAND

Prairie Orchid Co
515 Elmhurst Rd
Winnipeg, MAN R3R OV2 CANADA

Don Raum
53 River St
Boston, MA 02108

Richella Orchids
2881 Booth Rd
Honolulu, HI 96813

Schreiber's Orchids
Zephyr, Ontario L0E 1TO
CANADA

Soroa Orchids
15851 S.W. 198th Ave
Miami, FL 33187-1032

Stewart Orchids
P.O. Box 550
Carpinteria, CA 93013

Stones River Orchids, Rt 5
Box 262, Clovercroft Rd
Franklin, TN 37064

Tropical Temptation Orchids
217 So. Bowman Rd
Chillicothe, OH 45601

Vacherot & LeCoufle
30 rue de Valenton BP8
Boissy St Leger, 94471 FRANCE

Van Horn Orchids
1316 Peden
Houston, TX 77006

Waldor Orchids
10 E. Poplar Ave
Linwood, NJ 08221

W.C. Orchids
1389 Friends Way
Fallbrook, CA 92028

Orchids by Wilson
1827 Ahrens
Houston, TX 77017

Zuma Canyon Orchids
5949 Bonsall Dr
Malibu, CA 90265

Section 22. Bibliography

Batchelor, S. 1981 Orchid Culture—Fertilizing
Amer. Orchid Soc. Bull. 50(10): 1208

Batchelor, S. 1982 Orchid Culture—Diseases, Victims of Virus
Amer. Orchid Soc. Bull. 51(7) : 719

Batchelor, S. 1982 Phalaenopsis—Part 1.
Amer. Orchid Soc. Bull. 51(12) 1267-1275

Batchelor, S. 1983 Phalaenopsis—Part 4.
Amer. Orchid Soc. Bull. 52(3) 244

California Fertilizer Assn. 1975
Western Fertilizer Handbook C.F.A. Sacramento, CA

Cooperative Extension, Univ. of Calif. 1985
Water Quality and Its Effects on Ornamental Plants #2995

Curry, R. 1975. Mesophyll Collapse in Phalaenopsis
Amer. Orchid Soc. Bull. 44(6) : 497

Dourado, F. 1978. Phalaenopsis Violacea of Malaya.
Amer. Orchid Soc. Bull. 47(8) : 699

Freed, H. 1979. The Practice of Breeding
New Horizons in Orchid Breeding   HF Malibu, CA

Goh, Straus and Arditti. 1982. Flower Induction and Physiology in
Orchids. Orchid Biology: Reviews and Perspectives, II (Ardittied)
Cornell Univ. Press, London

Griesbach, R. 1983. Orchid Flower Color—Genetic and Cultural
Interaction. Amer. Orchid Soc. Bull. 52(10) : 1056

Griesbach, R. 1984. The In Vivo Propagation of Phalaenopsis
Orchids. Amer. Orchid Soc. Bull. 53(12) : 1303

Koopowitz and Kaye. 1983. Plant Extinction: A Global Crisis.
Stonewall Press, Washington, D.C.

Langdon, W. 1980. R Values. Moveable Insulation p. 26.
Rodale Press, Emmaus, PA

Mazuria, E. 1979. Natural Processes. The Passive Solar Energy
Book. p. 26. Rodale Press, Emmaus, PA

McCorkle, J., L. Reilly, and T. O'Dell, 1968. Pseudomonas   Infection
of Phalaenopsis. Amer. Orchid Soc. Bull. 38:   1073-1078

McCorkle, J. 1971. Comments on Certain Infectious Diseases of
Orchids. The Orchid Digest Vol. 35, No. 8.—Oct 1971.

McCorkle, J.D., and J.M. McCorkle, 1974. Bacterial Sheath
Infection Due to Pseudomonas and Practical Aspects of
Control. Amer. Orchid Soc. Bull. 43: 780-782

Nelson, P. 1981. Insect Control. Greenhouse Operation and
Management. p. 411. Reston Publishing, Reston, VA

Poole and Sheehan, 1980. Mineral Nutrition for Orchids.
Orchid Biology: Reviews and Perspectives, (Ardittied)
Cornell University Press, London

Peters Fertilizers, 1981. Peters Fertilizers: Sales Manual.
W. R. Grace and Co.

Ricket, H. 1957. What Makes Plants Flower? Botany for
Gardeners. MacMillan Co., New York

Salisbury, F. 1971. The Biochemistry of Flowering. The Biology of
Flowering. p. 132. Natural History Press, New York.

University of California, Cooperative Extension, Flower and
Nursery Report, p.1, Spring, 1982.

Valmayor, H. 1984. Flowering Seasons of Philippine Orchids,
Orchidiana Philippiniana, Volume 2. p. 298-300.
Samhwa Printing Co. Ltd. South Korea

White, J. 1985. Considering New Sources. Florists Review.
176(4544) 37-41.

Section 23 INDEX

For additional copies of Culture of the Phalaenopsis Orchid write:

Laid-Back Publications
276 East Shamrock
Rialto, CA 92376

1990 price $19.95 postpaid. Price subject to change without notice.
California residents include 7% state sales tax.